RUBBER ROOM

ROMAN

A NOVEL

EVERYTHING YOU NEED TO KNOW AND ASK
ABOUT THE EDUCATION SYSTEM

CINDY GROSZ

Motivational PRESS®
LEADERS IN GLOBAL PUBLISHING

Published by Motivational Press, Inc.
1777 Aurora Road
Melbourne, Florida, 32935
www.MotivationalPress.com

Manufactured in the United States of America.

ISBN: 978-1-62865-255-0

Contents

WHAT IS EDUCATION????

"Educating the mind without educating the heart is no education at all."

— Aristotle

"Tell me and I forget. Teach me and I remember. Involve me and I learn."

— Benjamin Franklin

"Education is not the learning of facts, but the training of the mind."

— Albert Einstein

"Education is the most powerful weapon we can use to change the world."

— Nelson Mandela

HAVE YOU HAD YOUR CHARACTER QUESTIONED????

"The ultimate measure of a man is not where he stands in moments of comfort and convenience, but where he stands at times of challenge and controversy. "

— Martin Luther King, Jr.

PREFACE

If you are reading this page, congratulations!!! You have embarked on an adventure that will ultimately affect your thoughts about education, politics and history. *Rubber Room Romance* is the first book of its kind: part novel – realistic fiction – part factual discussion and all questioning the education system we have today.

I am told by many that I am somewhat intelligent. I am an accomplished marketer and promoter. I am also an educator, having earned an award for my teaching and accomplishing high scores on NYC state tests. I am a mother and a taxpayer. I watch television and read all types of materials about education. I am surrounded by so many who consider themselves "intelligent" as well. Yet, none of us have what it takes to answer the following question – "What is wrong with our education system today?"

My goal in this book is to bring attention to a problem that affects all of us. The fictional part of my book is based on real people and settings currently ongoing and "covered" in the media in such a way that makes a common person angry and frustrated. This book is for the reader who reads for entertainment AND also for the one who works in education, follows politics and government and wants to work with others for change.

This book is for the mother who speaks English as a Second Language and for the homeschooling parents in a rural setting. This book is for a college student thinking about making education a career, and for the grandparent who doesn't get that they are paying for education everyday in many ways. This book is for those in book clubs that compare characters, infer ideas and relate their own experiences.

My goal is to engage conversation. My desires are for people to actually research details and learn to speak with others to create ideas based on facts and share them in a positive way.

This book is NOT about me. My story is my story and I will not discuss the facts surrounding my situation. Opponents will share their version, supporters will tell a version of their own. Use MY novel and the sections afterward to see if any of the information makes you question what you think you know.

I would like to think of myself as part Danielle Steel or Jackie Collins, part Sandra Feldman. I want to be a trailblazer in entertaining while being an activist for quality education for all ages, all backgrounds, and all people. A strong education system leads to a better economy, more jobs and positive immigration reforms. A strong education system helps end anti – semitism, racism, bullying and depression and crime/violence. Most importantly, a successful education system brings America back to its "super world power" status.

Again, *Rubber Room Romance* is a novel of fiction. Because it is set in New York, names of real organizations and public figures seemed to fit the story best. The main characters and their situations are from my creativity ... and any resemblance to people you seem to know are simply coincidental.

As we went to press, Jackie Collins passed away. "If you want to be a writer, stop talking about it and sit down and write!" Was one of her most famous quotes. I listened. Thank you for your words of wisdom and for teaching me all about "Chances."

Cindy Grosz

RUBBER ROOM ROMANCE

THE NOVEL

CHAPTER 1

"Mark, Mark ... the baby is crying."

Mark was so engrossed in his usual routine of drinking a cup of coffee and reading the newspapers that he did not hear his own child wanting his attention.

"Mark, I'm in the bathroom ... please ..."

The phone rang. But the distraction of the phone alerted Mark of the shrills coming from the baby's crib.

He went to pick up the baby.

Standing and cuddling his baby, Mark could not believe the joy and peace he felt given what he had gone through the past few years.

"Wow, what a beautiful sight," Sarah remarked as she walked towards each of them and moved to give each a kiss.

"I'm going to call Ellyn and ask her and Michael if they want to meet next weekend for dinner."

"Should I make breakfast?" Sarah continued talking as she left the room, grabbed her own coffee and starting to sit and read the paper Mark had left on the kitchen table.

"Mark, Mark did you see this?"

"Teacher investigated after complaints about teenagers drinking in their home at a prom party," Sarah starting to read aloud with an expression of that had an Oh My God about to come afterward, when Mark interrupted ..."

"Check out the news, they have two pages of stories that totally conflict, schools short – staffed and then another about how much money is being paid by the city to ATR or subs,"

"Just another day in paradise ..."

The phone rang again. This time Sarah didn't wait and within the second ring picked up the phone.

"Hello, Oh hi, Melissa, funny you called."

Some seconds of silence.

"Yes, we saw, but from what we know firsthand, nothing surprises us anymore."

From Melissa's end, "And then they wonder why nobody wants to be a teacher or principal anymore."

She continued, "But the real reason I am calling is because it seems like a beautiful day. I thought we could meet in the park by the playground and have a picnic."

"Sounds like a plan," Sarah said. "Does 12:30ish work?"

"Perfect," responded Melissa and then asked to go so she could do some work before meeting.

They hung up and Sarah returned to the baby's room where Mark was in the rocking chair, holding the baby and pointed to a picture in a book he was reading, the baby's eyes engrossed at a colorful rainbow."

"And do you know what comes after a colorful rainbow ..."

"Mark, that was Melissa, we are all going to meet around 12:30 in the park."

"I have to meet someone around 11:00, but as soon as I am done, I will grab a cab and join you. Didn't you me mention something before about calling Ellyn."

"So you were listening to me," Sarah said with a smile.

"I always listen, and I will especially listen to you tonight ... after the baby is asleep."

"Funny, and I recall I time when confiding and listening to me were like ... poison.

"I'll share with you my poison anytime," Mark joked ... and smiled.

"Thank god you can laugh at it now ... not so long ago there was a time when ..."

Mark interrupted her, "Please don't ruin my trying to be romantic husband moment by bringing THAT up."

"Ok, but about that poison later ... and she went over and shared a long, passionate kiss with him.

Mark didn't want it to stop but knew he had a meeting to attend shortly with a potential new business connection.

Mark reminded Sarah, "Call Ellyn, we haven't seen her and Michael for quite a while ... let me get ready." And he gave both Sarah and the baby a peck on the cheek and he proceeded to the closet, grabbed a towel and walked toward the shower that was already running.

Sarah carried the baby to the den, put the baby in the portable pen and grabbed her cell to call Ellyn.

"Hi Ellyn, Sarah."

Ellyn responded, "I have been meaning to call Mark and Melissa. How are you?"

"Mark and I thought we should make plans soon. How is Michael? The kids?"

"We are all great, but before I get personal ... I want to ask you something serious. Several teachers from my community and from different schools are concerned about their evaluation status and want me to advise them informally about what I know ... and if Mark had the time ..."

Sarah cut her off, "Ellyn, Mark is finally over the whole fiasco, so for me ...I would say no, but Mark would never say no to you or to a teacher in need."

Then Sarah continued, "Have you been reading the papers?"

Ellyn answered, "Yes, and cable has been running stories nationwide about educators ... that prom story ...what makes a teacher any different from any other professional from kids sneaking alcohol at their home on their time ...they would have to arrest half my neighborhood, if not more?"

Sarah responded, "Yeah, kids admitted they brought the booze, it was being served."

"Anyway, the whole story makes me sick, so I hope you and Mark are in."

"Let's talk about it more when we meet," Sarah answered, they then proceeded to make plans for dinner the following week.

"Who would have ever thought during those days at New York University we would be in the position we are in today," Ellyn said.

"What, superheroes for educators, Can I be *Catwoman* and claw my nails down a blackboard,"

Ellyn interrupted, "As long as I am not the *Lone Ranger.*"

"Funny ... I think we are more like *The Avengers* and with that I must hang up and change a diaper."

Sarah got off the phone and updated Mark on the conversation.

"Yes, New York University students save the Board of Education ... that has a nice ring to it even if we never started out that way."

And, as Mark said that, he looked at the picture of the "three amigos" at their graduation, sitting in a "friends forever" frame all three bought together recently and proudly displayed in each of their homes.

CHAPTER 2

It was midmorning on a blistering hot June day, and the air was full of caps thrown into the air in jubilant celebration. For staff and faculty, it was just another graduation. For the hundreds of seniors moving up the ladder, though, it was excitement, chaos, and dreams of love, money, health, and altruism. This was especially true for Ellyn, Mark, and Melissa.

Three best friends were standing next to each other, pushing others away, and pulling at clothing that was making them uncomfortable. Their parents, grandparents, and siblings took turns snapping photos, poking cameras in faces and waiting for just the right smiles, hugs, and kisses. This picture would prove fill one montage of their story, sitting in each of their homes in matching frames more than a decade later.

Mark and Melissa had met accidentally in their last school year.

"Excuse me," said an embarrassed Mark as he was walking backwards away from a shelf with an armload of books. He banged into a studious classmate holding an equally impressive stack that dropped immediately to the floor, and even hit his toe in the extremely large Bobst Library. At the center of New York University's area for study and research, it was a place where all had to go, wanted to go, and even went for a scenic view to look through the famous Washington Square Park archway up Fifth Avenue.

"Let me carry your books back to your table," Mark said, with a quirky smile that shy Melissa connected with. Melissa accepted Mark's offer, but as they were unsuccessfully trying to whisper, they were asked by a library staffer to please take their discussion outside.

They quickly became friends and started to going school parties and organization meetings together. When Melissa started dating one of the reporters of the school's newspaper, she turned to Mark for "boyfriend" advice when she felt frustrated.

Melissa was investigating student employment opportunities when she met Ellyn. Melissa was waiting her turn in the waiting room by the school employment office during her freshman year that April. She couldn't help but notice the organized list of questions and notes on the pad sitting on the lap next to her. She suddenly felt insecure, intimidated and maybe as if she had missed the memo about bringing this information to her meeting.

"Wow, you're prepared," Melissa commented to the other girl.

"Well, I really need a job and don't really have the time to actually look, I'm hoping to get interviews and hired soon. I'm Ellyn Postin. I think you are in my mythology analysis class."

"Melissa Dobbs – and yes – I think every freshman takes that class since it requires only one paper, one test and most seem to get A."

They chatted another fifteen minutes until Melissa was called into her consultation. "Here, take my phone number and call," Melissa said as she jotted down her number on an index card and gave Ellyn a friendly smile.

They met for lunch after class the following week, and soon became friends. Ellyn was commuting at the time, and as they became closer, she began to stay in Melissa's dorm room for late parties, all – night study sessions and just "girl – time." Through Melissa, Ellyn met Mark and his friends, and Melissa met Ellyn's fiancé.

Ellyn had met Michael Marks at a sweet sixteen; she soon knew that wherever their paths would lead, he would eventually be "the one," and she and the future Dr. Michael Marks dated throughout their years at New York University. After graduation, Michael would be starting at New York University's Dental School that summer, while Ellyn was soon to start a sales job at St. Barth's jeans, the country's largest pants manufacturer.

Ellyn, Mark, and Melissa all had plans, that hot June graduation day, and they would all go their separate ways, for a while.

For a while.

CHAPTER 3

A few months later, Mark and his younger brother Nathan were double dating at a new "chic" restaurant where through family connections they were able to reserve a great table without waiting, despite a write – up in the New York Times only weeks before creating lasting unavailability for the general public. The brothers broke the usual "bro – code" and jointly went to the men's room together shortly after the waiter took their orders.

"What at nice night," Mark's date Cassie mentioned to Lindsay, Nathan's date and recent interest.

Lindsay responded without Cassie realizing she was being tested. "What do you like about Mark?"

"Well, he certainly knows how to enjoy life and spend money," laughed Cassie, and with that Lindsay had her answer.

The brothers were just returning to their table when a loud crash brought the entire dining area to a complete halt. Apparently, a child had run into a busboy with a full load of dirty dishes and somewhat – filled drinks, completely crashing all to the floor and barely escaping injury. The patrons sitting near them jumped back with a clamor of "What have you done here? Look at my new suit! Where is the manager?" as another ran to the bathroom to clean himself. An elderly woman got up to try to help clean, dampened her napkin, and knelt on the floor to wipe around the waiter's cut, where blood was gushing out.

Chaos continued for the next few minutes, but Mark strode quickly to the boy, who was screaming and crying hysterically. "Don't worry," Mark soothed the child, "I see this happen all the time." Mark cuddled the boy and began to wipe him with a wet napkin.

The parents were trying to explain to the owner of the restaurant that their child had some disabilities. They offered to pay for any expenses, but Mark interrupted with, "It has been taken care of." Mark sat on the floor with the boy paying attention to him and gradually calming him down. When the parents thanked Mark, his only response was a smile and "Enjoy the rest of your night."

Lindsay and Cassie were watching the whole series of events when Cassie blurted out, "Why did he do that?" "Because Mark is just a nice guy and someone who cares," Lindsay responded, and with that they continued their dinner. Cassie never saw Mark again.

Mark's loyalty carried in every area of his life.

Mark had gone directly from that graduation day at New York University into his family's discount stores business, which also included many real estate holdings, but that was never his long – term goal. Mark's father and his two brothers were immigrants, born in Europe. They entered the United States with the hopes of achieving the "American Dream." During the 1970s, and the growth of discount chains selling copies of designer jeans, halter dresses, and lavish accessories, the three brothers were able to borrow enough money to start successful stores in all five boroughs and keep a small real estate business on the side, being known as fair and friendly building owners.

Mark had five male cousins and three female cousins. They were a close family, and it was expected that all the wives of the siblings and the children got along. All vacations were taken together. All the children went to the same schools, camps, and after school programs. Every family gathering was planned with everyone together, and at alternating homes so that the respective other sides and close friends would be able to share in the festivities.

His eldest cousin went to study in a collegiate program overseas and met a girl who shared his desires to help others in need, never settling on a native home or having children. "My homeland is wherever my heart is," he proclaimed when he felt the need to defend himself from often nosy, gossipy people.

Nathan and Mark were closer than ever during Nathan's senior year of high school. He was already accepted to New York University's business school on full scholarship like Mark. On night as he was getting walking around the back of his car, a drunken driver swerved onto the driveway, running Nathan over and killing him instantly.

On the afternoon of Nathan's funeral, Mark sat at his desk for a time daydreaming what he thought his future with Nathan would have been like; his plans for the future. Nathan, he was thinking, "Oh Nathan, what a team we could have been.

Now Mark was sitting at his desk, staring at the picture of the brother he and his grieving parents had just buried. It just isn't supposed to be this way, he was thinking. Nathan had already begun working part – time in their family's business, learning with a natural, joyous talent the ways to deal with suppliers, becoming a "natural" at negotiating with employees to find ways to increase productivity and encourage hard work with a visible reward system. "What a future you had waiting, Nathan. What a future." Mark sighed to himself.

Sitting at his desk that afternoon, trying to absorb sense of loss, Mark realized that Nathan's involvement in the family business had meant Mark had options, choices, including graduate school to obtain an MBA. With Nathan gone, those options were closed. He closed the MBA application file sitting on his desk and put it into a drawer. Then, he returned to the grieving family joining in the living room area.

His cousin, Isabella, joined the business on the same day he did. While he was out generating business, focusing on making sure each store was well stocked, managed with tight security, and meeting new contacts for inventory distribution, Isabella was given a "fluff" job with a title calling her "media" observer. They received the same starting salary and benefits, while producing a different quality of work. Mark resented it, as did his father, who was well aware of the situation. He could do nothing, since it was his niece, his oldest brother's daughter, and as everyone thought, she would soon marry, have babies and all would end up sharing the entire corporation evenly.

Isabella did nothing to honor her old – fashioned family. She partied late almost every night. She consumed several drinks and tried drugs routinely. Worst of all, she began sleeping with many men with whom her family did business, and she became the gossip of the entire business and social community her parents were involved in. Within six months, she was back at home, studying for a social work degree at a local school for her masters. She was introduced to a nice young medical student from California, and under her parents' strict guidance was engaged within three months.

Mark was fulfilling his father's and uncles business dreams for him. Within a year, he proved his value, offering younger, innovative ideas and more diversification. However, Mark was not truly happy. He missed academia. He was lonely without his younger brother. He dated, but nothing seriously since college. He met with friends, but in the end felt very lonely. He knew that he could not do this the rest of his life. He also was aware he could not intentionally hurt his family. So much was riding on his shoulders.

So much.

A special surprise was carefully planned for Mark's 23rd birthday. His parents planned a small dinner at home with just his immediate family; this meant his aunts, uncles, and first cousins – and of course, his nana, the only grandparent still alive, his mother's mother. Food was brought in from his favorite restaurant, served on the best china by hired help.

After everyone left, Mark's parents ushered him into the den, offered him a drink, which he refused, and gave him a big box, telling him that they needed to talk about this gift.

Never being one to mince words, Mark's father led him to the couch, sat across from him on a second couch with his wife, and began to suggest immediately to open the gift. Mark tore the paper slowly, as to not to make a mess, and saw the box was plain white, with no hint of the contents inside. He looked confused at his parents, when his mother told him to open the box and see what was inside. He did as he was told, and to his amazement was another box, and this went on until he finally opened the smallest box with a card in it. Just a card, telling him to enjoy his birthday and continue to grow to be a man that they are so proud of. Not wanting to sound greedy, he thanked his parents for the lovely dinner and meaningful words.

"That is the son I have, too proud and classy to say what he really feels," said his dad, looking directly at him, cupping his wife's hands for support as he started to talk about what they had been preparing for weeks. "Son, are you happy?" he asked. Mark looked at them as if they were crazy.

Mark responded as any son would under these circumstances – that is, how lucky and grateful that he was for their love and devotion. His mother interrupted him and took over the conversation, getting straight to the point. They knew that he was not happy. Their gift was not a material possession, but instead a future. They offered to pay for a degree of his choosing to start a life that he desired, with hopes of meeting the right girl, getting married, and ensuring them plenty of grandchildren to spoil.

Mark was relieved and surprised by this gift. Mark also felt guilt, as he had to represent both their sons, regardless of whether or not they were alive. His shoulders felt heavy. During the next few weeks, he thought about his next move. He simply could not walk away, yet he knew he had to do something. Through conversations and careful thoughts, many lists and sleepless nights, he came to a conclusion; it was one that he thought would make him happy, one that was fair to all.

He did not hate the family business. Actually, he was quite good at it. Outsiders noticed, as did the business media and organizations. He made a decision, one that he thought would make all happy. He went to his parents' home, told his parents that he wanted to speak seriously, and all went directly into conversation.

Mark explained that he felt guilty about leaving everything, even moving out after returning after graduation. "I've decided to go to school, work and live at home, no apartment in the city, no high – cost education." Mark's parents told him to rethink, that they had plenty of money; they wanted him to be happy. The truth was, though, that Mark loved his family, his dog, and his home – and his connection to his deceased brother. He tried to see the pros of living home as meaning to not take care of an apartment and the biggest was keeping an eye on his parents.

Within six months, Mark was enrolled in the Master's program in Hunter College's Special Education program, with a guarantee for student teaching after graduation if he could graduate with honors.

He made an office out of an extra bedroom and was able to visit the main offices once a week.

Mark loved school even more than he thought he would. He really related to his fellow students and became friends with many of his professors. Many knew his family's reputation and secretly admired his tenacity for learning, working, and succeeding. The three years of study flew by, and Mark graduated with honors and continued to excel in business; he was actually able to help expand the real estate holdings of the entire corporation.

But the true success of his three years at Hunter was meeting the beautiful and smart Sarah Feldin. Sarah had grown up in Westchester, very much like Mark. Sarah's parents had liberal ideas and wanted their children to benefit from social and urban lifestyles, so they pushed all six children into academia.

Mark and Sarah married upon graduation, and both started teaching in schools in Manhattan. Mark purchased an apartment so they both had an easy commute and lived within walking distance of subway stations. They led a charmed newlywed lifestyle, having a honeymoon in Europe, frequenting local restaurants and enjoying many friends.

They seemed totally in sync, finishing each other's sentences, sharing meals, and even getting along with the in – laws. Mark got a weekend job coaching a local little league team. Both were happy, and their future seemed complete.

CHAPTER 4

It was a beautiful, fall, autumn night – the sky filled with cool, crisp air as many a single girl in their twenties would venture out with friends for fun, mingling and celebrating the end of a work week.

Melissa was debating to which movie she was going to go to. As she usually did, Melissa went alone. Her "date" would be Liam Neeson or a star from a serious drama getting great reviews featuring a group of British actors.

She was putting on her coat when her house phone rang. She was not about to pick it up until she heard the following," Ms. Dobbs, this is Stephanie's mom. She is having a hard time understanding the math problems you assigned her. Please call back." Before the sentence was finished, Melissa put down her bag and grabbed the receiver.

Melissa sat on her couch, and listened as the mother of one of her most troubled students went on and on about the homework. "Did Stephanie explain we draw our answers in class? ... Let me show you another example of how you can triple digit m ... I'm sure you never saw this before," To all their amazement, they went on talking for almost an hour.

And there went the movie. But Stephanie did earn a score of 90 on the following week's math test. Melissa saw the joy on Stephanie's face and felt pride like as if she were her very own.

An only child, Melissa had gone straight from New York University to Teacher's College at Columbia University for her Master's Degree. She had always wanted a big family and a career working with children, so in high school she surrounded herself with kids of all ages by volunteering at her local community center's tutoring program and working at camps each summer. She was frequently requested by parents to head their girls' groups.

She studied endlessly to reach Columbia, and once there, she loved her courses and professors in each teaching class. She became friends with the staff at Teacher's College and often did extra projects for her educators when they needed someone to visit a school or be part of a research project.

During her second year in the Teacher's College, Melissa started a teaching job at a small private school on the Upper West Side of Manhattan. Usually only graduates got these jobs, but Melissa's hard work and her friendships with the professors who respected her helped her to get the position in hopes that she would get hired there as soon as her Master's was completed.

Melissa spent her weekends developing lesson plans that amazed everyone. Senior professionals could not believe her originality, her connections to leveling lessons for individual students, and her ability to explain in her notes. In addition, her plans offered alternative ways to teach the same lesson if something suddenly changed, such as the students not connecting the ideas or a supply problem.

One day, she was called into the principal's office. She had no idea why. She had heard through the staff gossip pool that no one gets asked to the principal's office unless there is a problem.

She arrived 10 minutes earlier than asked, and sat by the closed door, waiting impatiently. The door never opened. Not even on the time requested. She did not dare say a word, not even to the secretary, whose loyalty to the administration was known in the building.

Melissa had brought one of her new purchases. Daydreaming, Melissa imagined that she was sharing the new reference guide with the principal and volunteering to run one of the after – school required professional developments.

Over the past few months, Melissa had led several sessions working with staff and received overtime pay and pensioned income, one of the "perks" of her contract and friendship with those in power.

"Ms. Dobbs, why don't you just take a seat ... I will escort you in when the principal is ready," the secretary mentioned in a cold, formal manner. "Aren't we formal today, Ms. Whitney," as Melissa turned back and sat down next to a total stranger, feeling quite out – of – place.

Melissa looked around – and everyone ignored her – not even as much as a wink. It seemed different, because, no matter how busy and crowded the room was, she would have her way. Melissa connected with everyone, especially the secretarial staff who overlooked protocol, allowing her to make copies, use a school phone or even grab some papers.

Melissa started to get up and walk towards one of the secretary's desk.

"Please sit and wait your turn."

Melissa was concerned. Five, ten, then fifteen minutes passed. She wanted to take her lunch, and her free time was running out. The bell rang, and still nothing. She said nothing.

What Melissa did not know was that the principal was not in there – intentionally. Finally, Melissa heard the secretary's phone ring, the direct buzz only from the principal. A few minutes later, the secretary got up, walked over to Melissa and summarized the message that she received on the phone conversation from the principal. Several apologies and a request to come to work one hour earlier tomorrow. Melissa was also told to take a full lunch hour and then return to her assigned classroom.

Simple and confusing.

The rest of the day, Melissa remained professional, but she was distracted. She cancelled an appointment after school, went straight home, ignored her phones, and went over the last few days in her mind. She reviewed all her notes.

The following day, Melissa arrived an hour and a half earlier than usual. Nobody was at school yet; the lights were out and several of the doors were still gated and locked. She sat on a step until she heard her name. It was her principal. She was pulling keys out of her handbag as she waved Melissa over to a small, more private entrance.

Melissa offered to help carry her belongings and then both proceeded to the office. The principal offered her coffee, but Melissa declined, and then both sat and the conversation began. "Melissa, you truly are a wonderful asset to our school, and everyone loves you, especially the students."

Melissa thanked her graciously for the compliments, and then the talk took a turn for the confusing.

"I understand you have many lesson plans. I would like to see them in their entirety. As a new teacher, your lesson plans need frequent review, so I need to see them. When can I have them?"

Melissa was confused and disturbed, but tried not to show it. In her most professional voice, she guaranteed her copies of the plans with all attachments by the end of the next school day.

The conversation ended, and still almost an hour before classes were to begin, they shook hands.

Before Melissa left, the principal in a casual tone suggested to Melissa that she should keep this meeting and conversation between them, even not mentioning it to her parents and friends. "You can't imagine how jealous some of the senior teachers would be if they thought I was favoring you," the principal explained.

The lesson plans were sealed in a box and handed directly to the principal as promised. Even the secretary had no idea of the meeting or plans being given.

Everything seemed to return to the status quo for the next few days.

CHAPTER 5

Things went on as if nothing happened at school for Melissa. Everyone was as friendly as ever, including the principal, who observed the official teacher in the class that Melissa was assigned to. Melissa was even invited to a baby shower for a senior staff member, the only new teacher so honored.

Finally, about a week after handing in the lesson plans, the principal saw Melissa in the hallway, and as if not planned, winked at her to get her attention. Melissa stepped to her, and the principal whispered, "I have some information for you, stop by before you leave."

Melissa stopped by as ordered. She was led by the secretary into the office and then sat while the principal was on a phone call. She sat and waited for ten minutes. The principal covered the receiver and apologized to Melissa for the call; it was unexpected and taking longer than she thought. She asked a big favor, coming in, again, early the next morning.

The principal was as friendly and unassuming as could be. She brought croissants, lattes, peppermint teas, and assorted fruits. Melissa was confused.

She started the conversation with chit – chat, asking how Melissa liked teaching, the school, her students ... all incidentals that were well known already to not only Melissa, but to anyone who knew Melissa. Melissa was getting an idea ... maybe she was offering her a job, a potential long – term position.

Then, the discussion went to the heart of the matter of the meeting – it was not a job in school. The principal wanted her lesson plans to use for professional developments, maybe more, but did not go into detail.

Melissa was filled with satisfaction, and a feeling of excitement: a position at one of the top public education elementary schools in New York City was eminent. Her hard work had paid off.

"Remember, Melissa, don't tell anyone, and I mean anyone, about any of this yet, you are still just a student teacher in training, others will be envious, even your family."

Melissa did not care what was told to her – she had worked hard, and her career was set.

CHAPTER 6

Ellyn and Michael Marks were married a week after that hot June graduation day. Their honeymoon, a gift from Ellyn's business friends, included a month on the corporate yacht, all expenses paid, stopping in Capri, Monaco, Greece and Turkey.

Ellyn, always a fashion maven, used family connections to get her initial interview and follow up meetings. The company hired only a "look" that fit the corporate brand and sent new employees to stylists, dietitians, and vocal teachers to make "cookie – cutter" representations to the world of their "family."

Actually, it was Michael's cousin who had the connection to the firm. At first, he was hesitant to have his future cousin work at a place known for its sexual and somewhat corrupt reputation. However, Michael and Ellyn needed the money, and Ellyn's dreams of future studies had to be put on hold. Ellyn started out as a paid intern, but celebrities and corporate connections liked her so much that within a few months, she was given the title "executive assistant to corporate personnel" – a glorified go – fer with all the benefits of respectability.

The next year was a year of growth for both in every aspect of their lives. Ellyn travelled extensively and was soon on the way to becoming a celebrity herself, often quoted in the business press updating information and trends. Michael was busy with classes, labs, and earning some money at a dental clinic.

Life was going well – in fact, very well – for the Marks the next few years. Michael's parents bought him into a thriving dental practice in Long Island, New York. Ellyn became pregnant almost immediately, and within six years, Maxie, Jonah and Lexi were born. She stopped working during her first pregnancy due to complications, but kept in touch with most of her staff and superiors and participated in events, parties, and meetings when she was invited.

Ten years flew by, and Michael bought into a bigger practice and combined six offices and twenty staff members into ten locations. Ellyn and Michael had bought a home on the North Shore of Long Island and a time share in Puerto Rico. She never loved anything more than being a wife and mother. She had never thought of herself as a nurturer, especially for children, but she enjoyed sitting in on toddler dance and sport classes and helping on trips and assembly programs.

Regardless of all her responsibilities, Ellyn found herself with more free time, and somewhat alone. Calls from college friends and business colleagues were fewer and far between. Invitations to exciting new events barely came. Ellyn's parents moved to Florida, as did Michael's, and neither needed their children for entertainment or help with health issues.

When Lexi entered kindergarten, Ellyn thought about going back to work – but as to where, she was at a loss. St. Barth's jeans had filed for bankruptcy in the mid – 1990s. When Ellyn made several calls to manufacturers and mentioned St. Barth's, she was politely told there were no positions open. Her disappointment led her straight back to homemaker.

Except for one topic, Michael and Ellyn usually got along marvelously. "Are we the lucky ones," Michael would often comment. He did not understand Ellyn's need to work. During a conversation late one night, Ellyn gave in to by ending Michael's chit – chat about her satisfaction by claiming, "Michael, you give me everything and more that should fulfill my dreams ... more than enough."

But it wasn't.

Ellyn had a degree. She felt the need to use it – and make her own money. Until the collapse of St. Barth's, Ellyn had made six figures with extensive benefits. She used to be quoted on page six of the New York Post and read the Wall Street Journal, Advertising Age, and Consumer Reports, for amusement as much as for business.

Ellyn never discussed her frustrations. Still, although Michael sensed something was missing in Ellyn's life, he did not know how to address or react to it. He also feared that she was bored with him. He feared that, if that was true, he would lose her. That frustrated him even more, because he took great care of himself, and though he was mature, he had become even better looking. Women hit on him regularly, especially after realizing he had a great income, status cars and watches, and worked out daily.

Most of his friends would consider such advances, and a very few even took advantage of them, but not Michael.

The day finally came, though, when Ellyn's frustrations forced their way to the surface. They were in bed, after a long passionate kiss, proceeded by caresses and tender lovemaking, when Michael got up and sat by the corner of the bed. There was total silence for long minutes.

Michael could not take it anymore. "What's up?" he said finally. "You seem distracted." He was trying to coax a conversation, thinking Ellyn would open up right away.

Ellyn responded that everything was fine, but he was not convinced and could not take it any longer. Ellyn never lied to anyone, not even to their kids.

Michael turned around and watched Ellyn put on her robe and step out of bed. He got up, put on his own robe and walked towards Ellyn, looking at her face – to – face.

"Sit down, Ellyn, we need to talk," and as he said that, Ellyn was worried that he was cheating or wanted a divorce, since he never spoke like that to her.

Michael spoke in a soft tone, and what started as a sentence went on like a speech, not even giving Ellyn space to say a word.

He sensed that something was wrong, he told her, and apologized if he did anything wrong, yet he did not know what he had done or said to lead to her unhappiness. "I love you more than anything. You seem so lost lately. Did I do something wrong?"

He even offered her a spa week away, saying that he would take some hours off to help the kids' carpools, homework, and whatever they needed.

All Ellyn could do was laugh, and loudly. She was shocked, amused even, thinking that Michael thought that he had done something wrong.

Ellyn calmed down and asked Michael, "Give me a few minutes, and I'll meet you downstairs."

Ellyn made coffee, met Michael by the table, cut up some fruit and sat down.

Ellyn started by summarizing a conversation that she had the day before with Sheri Bolinsky, her daughter's best friend's mother, while waiting for a dance class to end. Sheri had shared with Ellyn how the newest butcher in the neighborhood was selling sirloin steaks at chuck prices, and she had him cater a family dinner, and that it was the best meat that she had ever bought.

She stopped at that point, "Do you have any idea how I feel when this becomes a major topic of conversation?" Ellyn asked.

Michael tried to respond, to which he was totally lost. He finally opened his mouth.

"Are you having an affair?" was his only response, "Or do you want one?"

Michael walked out of the room to regain his composure.

He returned, and before anything was done, Ellyn just blurted out the truth: "I want to go back to school; I want to do something with my brain. I've looked in classes and am signing up for education classes on-line to get a Master's degree while the children are in school."

At first there was a bit of silence. Both looked down, especially Ellyn, since she wasn't sure Michael was up to hearing this – in her mind, he loved her as his "trophy wife," the woman who stood on his arm and helped him become the man he worked so hard to be.

Then Michael reached for her hand, caressed it softly, "Ellyn, you have been there for me in every step of the way to make our success.'"

Ellyn picked her head up, realizing she had doubted Michael and feared rejection for no reason.

He got up and leaned over the table to bring her body into his loving arms and warm chest.

"All this – it's nothing without you – you give me so much – now it is my turn – do what you must – and the children and I will help you with whatever you need."

"I was thinking about teaching – perhaps going for an advanced degree – at least being home holidays, summers."

"Think about how lucky those children will be to have such a caring adult in their lives – and how they benefit from what a great mom you are."

"Let's celebrate to a new step forward and a brilliant career as a teacher."

She and Michael dressed for lunch, went to the nearby diner, returned home, made love again, and then picked up their children.

Both were relieved; a better future was on its way.

CHAPTER 7

Ellyn put her mind to completing her Master's degree. In addition, she signed up for local courses, earning credits during the summer. They filled her morning schedule while the kids went to day camp. She woke each day at 5 a.m., worked out, arranged lists for the nanny and housekeeper, and wrote her schedule for the entire day.

Michael rearranged his schedules as well. He travelled less, made more money investing in real estate and the stock market, and invested in marketing, promotion, and advertising. He was asked many times to invest in retiring dental practices and to update them. He also had private training lessons and began weekly facials, manicures, and massages as advised by his image consultant.

Neither neglected their parents, friends, and most importantly their children or each other. That year, they did not take a vacation, using the time at home and adjusting the school days off with family, video movies, and game time. There were no play dates, shopping mall visits, or lunches out.

Adjustments were made, but during that year and a half, the family was never happier or closer. Ellyn and Michael did have some sacrifices, losing the opportunity for some organization work, social dinners, and free time to enjoy hobbies and leisurely reading, but overall, they were happy.

One morning, Ellyn woke up vomiting, thinking that she had caught one of the kids' colds, until several days later, she realized she was almost two weeks late. She was scared; the thought of becoming pregnant now was not only shocking, but unwanted. She had three children who were at the ages of developing independence, and the thought of sidetracking her education and future career were not happy thoughts.

After the kids were asleep, Ellyn as usual was reading something from her class on her hand computer. Michael had his own agenda, as he pushed aside the blanket from his side of the bed and crawled over to Ellyn. He put his arm around her waist to pull her over and started to nibble by her ear and lick her neckline.

Ellyn started smiling by the distraction, as her computer fell to the floor. They kissed passionately and then Ellyn caught herself as she realized she needed to speak with him about what she thought was an unexpected pregnancy. She started the conversation slowly, telling him about her assignment and how interesting she thought it was, and that her final project would be great in their oldest daughter's third grade class.

Michael knew Ellyn well enough to know that something was wrong; Ellyn would never forego some tender foreplay to a lesson plan.

"Now tell me what you really want," he responded as he sat straight up and looked directly into Ellyn's eyes.

Ellyn told him directly that she was pregnant. Michael was excited, both facially and vocally. He loved their family, money was not an issue, and he was already sure that they were having another boy, so the team would be even.

He stopped himself when Ellyn had no response, and was smart enough to realize this was not what she wanted.

"Do you want to abort?" Michael blurted out. This was a word never spoken in their home.

Ellyn did not respond at first, then replied that she would never give up on their family, but had other ideas – ideas that she would have to readjust to include diapers, midnight feedings, and redoing the newly finished guest bedroom into a nursery.

Two days later, Ellyn started bleeding. Her visit to her OB – GYN confirmed that she was never pregnant. She was just experiencing some change that could have been brought on by age, stress, change in a diet, or routine or anything else; it was quite common.

She was relieved. She had a goal, a timeline, and nothing could stop her now. She also changed her birth control, since she was healthy and able to become pregnant again.

Her cycle went back to normal within two months and the topic of having a baby or becoming pregnant never came up again.

Meanwhile, Ellyn was excelling in her classes, both online and on campus. Ellyn started putting together a resume, complete with a portfolio of lessons, photographs of classroom environments, and letters of recommendation from a variety of professionals, including former work associates and present mentors.

Ellyn started the foundations of looking for a job. Everyone thought that for Ellyn it would be a piece of cake – who wouldn't want her? Michael and Ellyn discussed her future employment. They agreed that she should not seek employment in any of the schools their children attended, or anything too close, for as Michael experienced time and time again, friends and neighbors take advantage of relationships, and often could not handle criticisms or the truth. Michael had the advantage of handing over those situations to colleagues in his office, but Ellyn would not. Once in her class, she would have little to no choice of changing a class, teacher, or grade, even if a parent was her friend.

She mapped out the school districts within a 45 – minute drive from her house and began the application process. She followed up the following three weeks with calls to hiring staffs and individual school secretaries.

To her amazement, she had few responses. She finally had her first interview with a principal looking for someone to take over for a teacher on sick leave. It was a four – month stint. Unfortunately, Ellyn would not have her license completed by then, and so in the mind of the principal, she met a nice woman, but it was a waste of time.

Ellyn went on several more interviews and sent out more resumes. She completed her studies with top grades, completed her extra courses and the state – mandated fingerprinting for official records.

Ellyn was called back to the original principal for a meeting.

"I called you back for a reason, because honestly, you remind me of my daughter. Let me give you some advice. Have you tried working for the New York City Department of Education?" She went on to explain that a woman of Ellyn's age was not likely to be hired. "The city is in short supply of teachers, while out here, we have an overflow, and when we need to hire, we get young out – of – college kids with no baggage at home and a youthful eagerness to fit in. They also cost less, and our benefits are less than those of the city."

"I will deny everything I said, so you didn't hear it from me. Go to Queens – there are so many openings all the time, and a woman like you, they'll worship."

The next day, Ellyn researched every school in Queens where she could teach. Within one month, she had six job offers for the following September.

She found out that, in the New York City school system, because of the union, her benefits would be better, her ability to save in a TDA would be better, and her tenure was guaranteed.

Ellyn finally got an interview for a small school teaching second grade about thirty minutes away, and with no connections to her family and friends.

The hiring administrator that Ellyn met was a lovely elderly woman who took a liking to Ellyn immediately. She explained that she would have to demonstrate several lessons to various board members and her immediate supervisors, as well as share a week – long log of lessons leveled for appropriate student groups, and how they would be adapted for students with learning disabilities and attention disorders.

Ellyn went through three days of intense observations, interviews, and meetings.

Meanwhile, at home, two other schools requested interviews to include Ellyn in their substitution pools.

Michael was extremely frustrated. Why wouldn't a person of Ellyn's caliber be of interest to top school districts in the nation? Ellyn, never one to have a hard time professionally, was upset, too. All the money, time, and effort with this kind of response?

CHAPTER 8

M elissa's routine at work stayed exactly the same. It was the spring, and plans for the following school year were being put into place. She was a little surprised to find out that in September there was going to be an opening since one of the teachers was retiring, and she was not even asked to participate in the interview process. Her school had a reputation for not only being a top – graded school, but one of the few schools the union favored as well. She made it her point to sit in on union meetings, befriend the staff union teacher representative, and even participate in union gatherings and phone banks and volunteer for handing out pamphlets for the elected officials they supported that election year.

She spent more and more time alone at nights and weekends. Friends were becoming fewer and fewer. Melissa was getting a lot of invitations to bridal showers, engagement parties and weddings, even a couple of baby celebrations. She turned every invitation down with a beautifully written excuse – already said "yes" to another celebration, going away that weekend, or a previous plan already made. She made sure not to use the same excuse one after the other, and especially for people that would have contact. In truth, she had no significant other, really had little in common and little communications over the past few years, and these invitations came with financial obligations that Melissa could not afford.

When her mother suggested she go to a couple of them and even that she would give Melissa money for the gifts, Melissa told her mother she had work obligations and could not go. "You are never going to meet anyone if you don't make the efforts," her mother would say over and over again, until Melissa stopped calling and her mother got the message.

Melissa would occasionally hang out for a burger and a glass of wine at the corner restaurant near her apartment. She met a "someone" very much like herself, except she was a legal secretary. They would sometimes go to a movie, grab a bite to eat, even talk about getting together and finding some place to meet nice guys.

Unknown to anyone, including her new acquaintance, Melissa was trying desperately to meet men via the internet. She went routinely on first dates, but very few called back after the meeting for coffee and look – see. Rarely did she get a second date, and if she did, the connection, or lack of, ended within two months.

Melissa was attractive, smart and likable, and the constant rejection made her feel ugly, not so intelligent and less happy – go – lucky.

Melissa's solution to fulfilling her time and interests was to remain focused on work, and work it was. One day, the union rep called her about a job offering in a school she was sure she could get her "through her connections" if Melissa was interested.

Melissa picked up her cell phone, "Oh hi, how are you? Wanna do a lunch tomorrow? I have a great idea to incorporate more teacher involvement with the next rally meeting."

"Melissa," the rep replied, "lunch would be good – my treat, let's to the salad bar – I'll drive, so meet me by my car."

Melissa fell asleep assured that she was on her way to becoming a school staff member and union representative with a wonderful mentor.

As soon as the bell rang, Melissa ran out the doors and to the car where the UFT rep was already in and the motor was on.

Melissa leaned in, gave her a friendly kiss on the cheek, and the car sped away.

"So I brought with me some notes about how some successful chapters are building staff momentum to rally against Albany about losing tenure," Melissa began to explain.

"Melissa, relax, let's get lunch and sit and discuss this then."

They parked, grabbed seats and ordered from the assembly line – the rep grabbed the check – and Melissa smiled, thinking to herself that it was token of gratitude for all her assistance.

They sat and Melissa started taking papers out of her portfolio. "Melissa, stop," the rep interrupted. "I have something to tell you." Melissa refused to listen, thought, and kept going on until finally the rep just blurted out, "You need to find a job elsewhere – the school is not hiring you for the September school year."

"What?"

"You're joking – very funny – is your way of telling me you want me as your delegate underneath you?'

"Melissa, listen – " and the rep's tone was so strong people surrounding them took notice.

"Melissa, there is a problem; there are no open spots for you."

"How could that be? Three teachers are retiring, and Terry promised me that I would be on staff since my first day here."

The rep didn't know what to say. "I tried, Melissa – I really spoke up for you; however, the staff is getting downsized, and you are the lowest on the seniority list."

"But I'm one of the best teachers in the school, and everyone knows that – even the union people. I simply don't get it."

"You know the contract better than most teachers – seniority over talent and success."

They went back to school. Melissa saw the principal deliberately turn from her – she knew about the lunch and conversation.

Apparently the job the rep had suggested "through her connections" was still available. Since Melissa wasn't sure about her future at her present school, she felt the pressure to say yes. It wasn't the level of this school, but Melissa needed job security for the fall.

Within two weeks, without as much as a phone call from the school administration, Melissa was hired to teach fourth grade, a testing grade, in fact the most important testing elementary school grade in the New York City school system.

She signed her appropriate paperwork. That summer, Melissa found a job tutoring and a summer camp position at a camp run within another school.

Alex Donovan was an executive for the summer program as part of his responsibilities at TWEED, the headquarters of the New York City

Department of Education. He would visit this site once a week as part of his overseeing several of the schools within the district he supervised. Melissa introduced herself on his first visit and gave him her phone number. "I am always available if you need some help on a program," she said with a big smile and reaching for a strong handshake.

He was everything Melissa was not. He came from a large family with six siblings and was raised by his grandmother and mother, and he worked for everything he had – at least that was his version of the story, and he was proud of it.

He was also a decade older than Melissa.

However, from their very first meeting, there was a spark between them, not necessarily a romantic one, but definitely a friendship. They exchanged numbers, spoke several times a week, and built a solid connection by the end of the summer.

Melissa prepared for her job in her new school all summer. She bought endless supplies, updated her lesson plans, set up all kinds of organizational materials for her "office" at home. She met for dinner with a couple of staff members from her old school and went on very few dates, discussing her new school, her old school, students in her class she loved and the cake brought in celebrating her ending her tenure as student teacher.

Maybe that was Melissa's problem – all she did was talk about school, school and more school.

Late one night, while on the phone with Alex, she suggested they meet the following weekend for a walk and picnic in the park. He brushed her off without any confirmation, and Melissa didn't take his rejection seriously as she continued to talk. The following week, Alex asked Melissa if she could stay late and fill bags for an upcoming event. She thought that he would be there. He wasn't, and his thanks came in a formal e-mail.

What Melissa didn't know was that Alex Donovan was a closet bi – sexual and did not have any romantic intentions with her at that time. He was seeing a man working in a hospital that he really liked.

She also didn't know that Alex Donovan had made up a resume to include a degree he never really had. He completed a GED and got his job through connections he made working summer jobs in his teens. He was handsome, groomed and knew how to talk and spend his money to get away with his story.

Melissa never brought up meeting again. It was months into her job when they grabbed a quick lunch and movie, and nothing sexual came between them.

CHAPTER 9

September came and went. So did October. Melissa had 23 students in her class. Luckily, her principal and co – staff welcomed her. They saw a young, eager teacher who wanted to be "a part" of them. She joined the social committee, volunteering to be a teacher representative at the parent – teacher – association meetings.

She had no social life. She worked until midnight and both days on the weekends on lessons, gathering materials, adjusting plans for individual students, even speaking to parents and guardians at all hours.

One night, she coincidentally looked online for a lesson plan idea, and as she googled, she saw something in disbelief.

Somehow, an anonymous educator was selling "HER" lesson plans under a bogus business – the same lesson plans that she had handed to her former principal months ago.

She called her old friend, the UFT rep. She would usually pick up her phone by the third ring, but this time it went to message center. When Melissa didn't near back from her, she tried later that night – and again got no response. She left a message: "Hi, It's Melissa. It is extremely important that you get back to me right away. Our friend, Alisa Whitney stole my lessons plans and sold them. They are online."

After a week of calls with no response, Melissa got a call from a union representative in the district office. "Ms. Dobbs, you have got to stop harassing a union rep in a school you are no longer in. This is a warning – one more complaint, and we are going to have no choice but to place you in a rubber room situation, and since you are not tenured, we will have no problem terminating you."

The district rep hung up and looked at the principal and union rep sitting across from her. "That should do it – you owe me, so remember when I call you to take a transfer teacher not to argue next time."

Melissa, confused and angry, called her neighbor, a legal secretary, and asked her advice. Within a few days, she heard back, and not with the answers she wanted.

She had no copyrights; she was a new teacher, and her former boss was a seasoned professional. It would cost her millions to fight in litigation, and the results would probably be something she would not like. She would look like a vengeful teacher who did not get hired for a job.

Based on the internet, they couldn't tie the administrator to the supposedly "bogus" internet seller anyway.

Melissa was convinced that the UFT representative that got her this current position was involved in the scheme to get rid of her as well, if not making money on the deal. Still, she had a job, she liked her situation, she was young and untenured, and she needed her salary and benefits.

She had no choice but to leave it alone.

CHAPTER 10

Ellyn's next few years flourished, both in and out of the classroom. Because she was so much different from the student body, she was intimidating. The community by the school was changing; there were more foreign – born families moving into the neighborhood. The staff was also changing, including many men and women from all over the world. Media and community groups spread the word that educators were needed, especially in the public school system. Many applied and were hired. Unexpected issues became clear. English was not their first language and they did not know the facts about American history. Math problems seemed confusing, as complex problems seemed impossible to solve – not to mention different currencies and measurement systems. Many of the seasoned aging staff members who lived in the suburbs and were enjoying the fruits of grand – parenting while taking care of their frail, elderly parents, were no longer treated with the same respect or knew the practices of the newer cultures they were involved with now. Ellyn's school represented a cornucopia of cultures and interests.

Ellyn stayed to herself, yet blended with all when she had to. Ellyn wore her designer outfits, but toned down the accessories and colors. She always wore simple, small heels and pantsuits.

Ellyn used her savvy to make everyone around her feel comfortable. She gave herself to each student, their families, and every staff member, including kitchen and custodial staff. Some spoke behind her back, criticizing her and making false judgments without basis, but for the most part, Ellyn loved teaching. However, once they got to know her, they gained respect for her. Ellyn loved working with people that were so different from her, telling people, "They are my teachers."

She always received satisfactory scores on her formal and informal observations. In fact, by her fourth year of teaching, she never received any sort of observation, even though documents were put in her file and her yearly review in June stated as much.

Her classroom was always used as the model for when visitors entered the building, whether the visit was announced or a surprise walk – through. Lenore Macy heard through the grapevine that Ellyn Marks was a great teacher – parents were visiting the office requesting her class for their children, her room was impeccable – and set up in a warm and inviting manner. She also had her name on several plaques hanging around the building.

Ellyn was eating lunch the way that she usually did: while working. Today, she happened to shut her phone so she could concentrate on the paperwork all Septembers brought with them. Making mistakes was not in Ellyn's vocabulary and carefully filing student records and cross – checking many documents took time and concentration. The more seasoned staff understood this well.

Ellyn got so engrossed within the first fifteen minutes that she actually forgot to get her lunch. She was sipping a water bottle when she heard a knock on the door.

She did not realize how long Lenore Macy been standing there, trying to get Ellyn's attention.

Ellyn got up and opened the door. After checking Ellyn's schedule, Lenore knew it was her lunch break. "I'd like to formally introduce myself, I'm Lenore Macy." Ellyn reached for a handshake and smile, and introduced herself as well. "Can we talk?" Ellyn did not want to hurt Lenore's feelings, but she wanted to complete the task already in progress. The parent advocate saw papers spread out and did not want to be pushy, but she did have a goal – to win Ellyn over.

Ellyn knew her lunch would be just as busy then. She also knew that she had to "play politics" and wasn't quite sure how to deal with her now. "Can I take you to lunch one day next week, my treat?"

They never got to have a complete lunch, but Ellyn did make sure to spend a preparation period with her that following Monday morning. Ellyn went through some personal background, compared notes of some professional experiences they shared, and the PA finally came right out and said it. "Mrs. Marks, I heard you were the best teacher in this school and I am hoping you will help me. I will do everything I can to help you."

When it became apparent that the Department of Education was having a problem with communication among its teachers, administrators, Department of Education staffers, community leaders, and most importantly, its parent body, parent coordinator positions were created specifically to serve within school buildings to resolve any tension stemming from a school environment that was a concern to families. Parent coordinators were the voice of the DOE for school activities, academics, available resources and the eyes and ears on all parties to create a comfortable school "family."

Once a parent coordinator is assigned a building, the coordinator tries to establish a harmony and trust. Smart and creative coordinators usually get a feel of who will help them the most, and in most cases, the best teachers with a strong parent following and reputation are their "go – tos."

They agreed that Lenore was to sit in Ellyn's class later that week and watch as she did a grouping of students for a reading lesson that would later relate to a school trip.

Because Ellyn was happy at work, her personal relationships also thrived. She managed to be the Parent – Teacher Association president at her children's elementary school, ran her temple's sisterhood, and arranged weekly deliveries for a food bank from Long Island restaurants for some Queens' outlets.

Her school was considered a top elementary school when Ellyn started there. During her fifth year of teaching, Ellyn led her grade in test score marks and was recognized by several organizations. To their credit, the four teachers on the grade received certificates from the school administration, district leaders and local politicians as a token of thanks. They also received several gift cards worth several hundred dollars each to use on school supplies and classroom needs.

Ellyn, being the person she was, added in a few thousand dollars and bought a computer system, complete with box speakers and upgraded internet systems, for her classroom.

Ellyn was asked to write the school blog once a month and she gladly volunteered. Michael and Ellyn were invited to many of the children's various religious and communal activities, and they always responded with a token gift card, and if available, attended.

While many would think Ellyn's home life would suffer, that was far from the truth. Her children were thriving in their own schools, friendships, and extracurricular activities. Michael's investments were paying off, and he upgraded his skills to develop a dental treatment for children with behavioral disorders so that medication would not interfere with any dietary or medical combinations. He travelled occasionally for dental seminars.

Travel was one of the few areas that affected Michael and Ellyn. In other circumstances, Ellyn would have joined Michael on these brief trips. However, the Board of Education was very strict about tardiness and absences. She also missed most of her own children's assemblies and had to make arrangements for various doctor appointments and after – school activity pick – up arrangements.

Otherwise, everything was going well, well enough for Ellyn and Michael to consider a bigger home in a tonier part of the North Shore and thoughts about buying land in Florida to build a second home.

Michael sometimes wished Ellyn would quit her job. Working for the Board Of Education was not that most glamorous job that the wife of a professional with his success would expect. He was aware that, behind his back, people would gossip as to why his wife worked, at "that kind of job." Ellyn never looked at her job that way, so he would never mention his concerns to her.

And now, they had their summers, since their children attended a sleep – away camp in Maine. They spent one month traveling.

August for Ellyn was typically spent updating her home, catching up with friends, and preparing for the fall, her children's schedules, and updating their wardrobes. She also spent a good amount of time preparing for her classroom and extending her social skills by organizing a unique event. Ellyn was the only teacher in her building to arrange a class reunion in the school's neighborhood and pay for the entire event. This year, she made plans for a class read – along at a Barnes and Noble and lunch for the students and two guests next door at Burger King.

Ellyn had to be told, informally, by her teacher friends that she was a fool. Nobody appreciated it; she was wasting her money, and if anything went wrong, parents would immediately sue her for any kind of excuse that a lawyer would persuade them to. She was also told that if the DOE, the Department of Education, wanted to, they could investigate and "give her trouble" by turning the event against her.

However, she never received any formal information, and she invited the principal, who somehow showed up at the very end of lunch and thanked Ellyn for a job well done.

There was always a pattern: Two weeks after the event, parents flooded the administration with calls requesting Ellyn as a teacher, even to have her change grade level and/or step up with the previous year's class.

So Ellyn never took her friends' words of wisdom seriously. They would never do anything to get rid of a woman who gave so much of herself to her school community and was recognized as a great teacher from those within the neighborhood.

Nine years of complete contentment.

CHAPTER 11

Nancy Johnson was 32 years old. She moved to New York, when she was 11 years old with her grandparents, who were both sickly. Ms. Johnson never knew her parents. She was the result of a one – night stand, and her mother died in childbirth. Her grandparents were lovely, hard-working people, making ends meet by taking endless positions as sales help in multiple jobs. They were involved in their church and were close with family members that lived in various states throughout the country.

Nancy Johnson took advantage of her grandparents. She cut classes, stayed out late, and did every kind of mischievous thing that she could to deal with what she felt were the "cards she was dealt." She never looked at all the good that she had, like the love and dedication of her grandparents, the food, clothes, and life in a nice – sized home attending decent schools for the most part staffed with quality teachers.

Nancy nearly died following a car accident on her way home late one night after working at a part – time job. A cousin living in North Carolina came up to visit her during her recuperation. Nancy's cousin mentioned that, if Nancy promised her and her grandparents to change her life, she would help her get a degree, a decent job, independence, and pride. Nancy was lying in bed, watching the only three people that she knew really cared about her giving her one last chance. "I know I have to change," Nancy finally admitted. "Don't you do anything – you are and will always be my love," her grandma said as tears of joy rolled down her cheeks.

Nancy recuperated and worked hard to make the changes she promised; she was able to graduate from an online college program and get a teaching degree. Nancy still had her wild side, but she made some positive progress. In fact, she continued living with her grandparents, mostly to save money, and to watch over them, as they were getting frail and more dependent on her.

Through her friends, she applied for the Principal Academy, built the right relationships, and found herself being offered a "plum" position without experience or interviews through the contractual obligations of meetings with the school leadership team.

Her immediate thoughts were about "being the boss." In fact, she was trained to think that way during her courses. She taught for one year, realized she did not like the classroom and interviewed for several administrator positions. While on interviews, she was given "valuable tips."

"Nancy, take advantage of the benefits the new contracts allow principals." "Nancy, you can get rid of a teacher you don't like if you work with your UFT rep," many of her colleagues would tell her.

Her own supervisor warned her that there would be those who would battle her authority and her rights and that teachers didn't have to respond to anything; in fact, according to the latest contract of the United Federation of Teachers, staff did not have to do a stitch of work until they arrived on the first contracted day of professional development, usually just days before or after the Labor Day celebrations, depending on the year and what day of the week it was celebrated on.

Nancy knew that she had to show her team who was number one. She was assigned to the building in early July and went into work every day to set up her office and get her support staff in place.

Principal Nancy Johnson introduced herself to the new staff via an e-mail in July.

Like most of the new administrators, Principal Johnson was a graduate of the Principal Academy. She had very little teaching experience; she taught for one year, and was told off the record to find employment of another kind.

So, when the staff got this e-mail in July, at first they connected informally, passed around all sorts of tidbits they heard "through the grapevine," and did not think much of it.

August 1st was always a monumental day for stores like Staples, Office-Max, and learning centers like Schooltime, where teachers bought their supplies and spent more than the allowances given through the dwindling Teacher's Choice, through the union. This practice of getting money would end during Mayor Bloomberg's administration.

Two weeks into the month of August, another formal e-mail came, from a new school heading on the stationary announcing that Principal Nancy Johnson was taking over. Ellyn was expected to touch base with her within one week.

However, like in any other profession, those who truly cared about teaching spent hours and days in professional development classes, extra credit courses, purchasing piles of supplies, and meeting socially with fellow staff.

Principal Johnson thought that her e-mails were "appropriate," but the union staff representative informed Ellyn and the others to disregard anything that came until further notice.

Some of the staff caved in, a few for fear, others for curiosity, but none took it too seriously until the first week in August. Everyone received certified mail – signed receipt packages. Not knowing what they were, they signed for the mail and then opened it in shock. They were to attend a day long meeting at a local diner and come prepared with a binder, highlighters, and willingness to work.

Clearly, this was a strict violation of the contract, and it was the expectable nerve of a novice administrator. Several staff were out of town, and a couple had summer jobs. Three people were working at summer school in other locations for the New York City Board of Education.

Calls flooded the union representative's phone. She responded that she was following up with UFT central offices, who in turn said they were "passing the buck" onto the CSA, or principal's union, to notify Ms. Johnson of her professionalism.

However, by August 5th, a reminder e – mail was sent to all reminding them of the meeting that they must attend on August 10th. There were no excuses allowed.

The union representative's only response was that union was working on it. But, as she said, they should all attend – as a "nice gesture" to illustrate unity. She stated that because they had signed for the packages that each had received at their home, Ms. Johnson could later use that against them.

Nearly all of the staff attended, and the few that did not had to prove validity for their reason for absence. Ms. Johnson made a point of mentioning in the meetings that all who did not attend were receiving letters in their file – again, another contractual violation. She also directed a warning to the representative, in front of everyone, not to attempt any grievances of any kind. Ms. Johnson had the union representative's number, and from that threat on, union representation in the school did not exist.

Teachers were arriving at all hours of the day during the last week of summer break in order to set up classrooms and have informal grade meetings to plan lessons together. While these were voluntary and informal, Ms. Johnson took it upon herself to visit and assign teachers extra work, like organizing school fundraisers, assemblies, guest visits, trips, and parent meetings. Some of her tasks again conflicted not only with the teacher's union contracts, but had potential violations of the NYCDOE's own code of rules – better known as the Chancellor's Regulations.

Nothing stopped Ms. Johnson. She became rude to students, parents, and school neighbors as well.

"Changes were taking place in all directions, let's see how the parents react," a teacher whispered to Ellyn.

CHAPTER 12

Mark started teaching in a school several subway stops away from his house and, from day one, found his niche. He was one of a handful of influential male teachers in the school. Because he had a business background, he brought to his lessons a different perspective than other teachers, both new and seasoned. He often joked with his wife and parents how he carefully organized his day for the "greatest profitability."

Mark had an office at home for his obligations to his real estate and family businesses, as well as cabinets labeled for his class. He loved sports, so coaching one of his school's teams was a project of love and pensionable income.

Mark went to the gym daily before school, met up with friends for a night out usually once every other week, and spoke daily to multiple family members. His first year of teaching was so successful that he became a union delegate voted in by his co – workers and helped develop a volunteer homework help program that met once a week.

He was a "guy's guy." But, because most of the staff were women, and several of them were not married or with significant others, he developed the skills to be sensitive to their needs and be a true friend.

Mark made it a point to communicate with his students' guardians routinely, even if to simply say hello, praise a good test score, or mention something positive that their child did in social as well as academic endeavors. Many of the students and their parents grew to depend on Mark for support, since many of the students were either local kids that had nannies to take care of them while both parents worked or students who lived in the outer boroughs, whose parents barely spoke English, yet stressed education and chose this school to best fit their child's needs.

Mark helped these parents as well, guiding them to get schooling through online or community – funded programs. The reality was that Mark was a teacher far beyond his student roster.

Within a few years, Mark's name quickly became a school "celebrity." His team was winning championships, and his name was known throughout other schools in the district.

Mark kept his personal life very private. Many were not aware he was married, nor had come from a prosperous family business that he was still active in. He was one of a few teachers who did not use the school computer or a cell phone for personal uses. When he was at work, he had one life, and, at home, he had another. "I live a lifestyle many that I associate wit could never relate to, I want them to think I am one of them," he would tell Sarah when she inquired why they didn't socialize with many of his work friends.

"Very few run a successful business too," she would respond. "Exactly," was Mark's last word and then they would move on.

Occasionally, someone would ask him if he would be interested in being fixed up, and when he continually said no, some questioned his sexuality. He knew this, but did not care. He was also careful on marketing and media exposure, and while he participated in school social events like the annual holiday party or end of year celebration, he never drank, stayed too long, or brought his spouse.

Mark did not have family pictures on his desk, nor did he wear his wedding band. He never drove his Mercedes convertible anywhere near the school.

"Ouch," yelled Sarah from the kitchen as she cut pieces of lettuce on the cutting board. The blood was flowing, and the cut was deep.

Mark ran into the kitchen, grabbed ice and a cloth, and tightly surrounded the cut with an intense grip. Sarah was not clumsy, nor was she one to complain. If she had yelled that loud, she was hurting. Mark knew it.

Mark just could not resist. She looked so sexy with her long flowing hair, natural looks with little makeup, and long lanky arms being surrounded by his muscular upper body. He twisted her around, as if there was no blood, no towel as it fell to the floor, no wedges of lettuce, cucumber shells that were recently scraped, no tomato seeds, and no avocado pit. As they turned and embraced, some of the garbage was slipping casually unto the floor. Yet to Mark and Sarah, they saw nothing, nothing except each other.

They made love on the kitchen floor, on top of and surrounded by dinner and blood.

They got up, realized they were famished, showered together, quickly dressed, and ran downstairs to eat at Danby's, one of the city's hottest restaurants. For most teachers, dinners at restaurants like this were beyond their budgets and did not fit into their salary. However, for Mark and Sarah, because Mark had supplemental income and Sarah worked, they were able to enjoy the city's best benefits. Their apartment was in a concierge building, and they had a status car parked in the garage building and were able to eat at upscale restaurants.

They also had no children and knew that, sooner or later, these spur – of – the – moment ideas to go out were numbered.

Danby's made the best guava martini, with a twist from their secret homemade simple syrup. They each had two drinks, shared appetizers and salads, finished with cappuccinos and returned home.

CHAPTER 13

September for the staff of Ms. Nancy Johnson was terrible. Such was life for the students and their parents. The DOE, New York Board of Education, received multiple complaints about the new principal through e-mails, letters, phone calls, and even visits by desperate parents whose children were being misplaced in classes and not getting the appropriate transportation. Many complained about confusions with the new routines set in place and the cold feeling they felt when they entered the building hallways.

People were complaining all over: the immediate district office, local elected officials, the investigative offices of the Department of Education, better known as OSI, or the Office of Special Investigations, and the SCI, the Special Commissioner of Investigations.

What people did not realize was that all of the departments had one boss, and that boss was the mayor. The mayor simply did not want to look bad.

When Ellyn submitted her first article for the school newsletters, something that she had routinely done for three years, she received a nasty note in her box. She basically had to rewrite the entire feature. She was even told what to write, even if the facts were somewhat exaggerated, if not total lies.

"Why don't you just give it up, you do it as a nice gesture ...you don't need the aggravation, nor the unappreciative attitude," Michael said to Ellyn,

However, Ellyn always looked at the glass as half full. She said that she could not let her fellow staff, but most importantly her students and their families, down. Ellyn kept in touch with many of the previous students and their families as well, as they depended on her for support.

Ms. Johnson started observations and write – ups on the first day. In fact, it seemed like that was all she did. Parents claimed that she never returned calls, nor did she keep her appointments. It seemed as if she knew little about the curriculum, nor had any idea how to set up the power points she wanted to use during the first two days of school.

Ms. Johnson made it a point not to say hello or get into any small chit – chat with her staff. Her secretary was under strict instructions never to interrupt her during a phone call or when her door was closed, which was turning out to be most of the school day.

The two assistant principals and the dean of the school, all seasoned professionals, had no choice but to follow her lead. Unknown to the staff, Ms. Johnson told them all privately that under no terms they were to give her any problems. They were all easily "replaceable," especially under the terms of the new administrators' contracts, which, for the first time, gave principals authority like never before and lucrative financial gains, but at the cost of their own tenure.

The UFT school representative was threatened as well. As in most schools, because of the time reps needed to help staff and attend union meetings, and because they often had seniority in their buildings, union representatives and the delegates often had "easier" schedules. That would mean being a "cluster" teacher with no classroom, or actually helping in reading and testing. These were "plum" jobs for many reasons.

"Send me a note, and I'll address the issue with the principal," was the standard line given to anyone who voiced a concern, at least in Ellyn's school. However, this seemed like something they were trained to say.

More and more union representatives faced this same dilemma. They wanted to keep their own jobs. There was nothing contractually that said the union "mouths" within each school building had to have these positions. They could be placed in classrooms, even the worst – behaved classrooms; as long as they could fulfill their duties, and administrators arranged appropriate coverage for them, they could "suffer."

So, help from the union disappeared. The Queens office sent in someone to meet the staff as if to appease them, but offered no concrete solutions. The best solution that they could offer was that "things were being looked into," and a reminder to support their union.

The first six months were to get worse. Ellyn finally gave up the newsletter just before the holiday season after being ridiculed and harassed about a voluntary project. Three students in her class asked for emergency transfers, and about 20 students within the building left.

"I can't take this new principal; she is going to ruin my daughter," Ellyn was told by one mother. "My son complains daily about how the principal makes demands for him and his friends to salute her as they walk by her ... I never heard of this."

One teacher transferred to another school in Brooklyn – a school with issues of academic and social deficiencies, but with administration that appreciated quality staff that was willing to work. When the teacher was willing to add two hours for her commute and share her fifteen years of experience, the principal jumped at the chance, and the teacher's transfer was made within a week.

Another teacher, after teaching for over 30 years and still being considered one of the best, secretly met with retirement consultants within the union. She was leaving in April, based on the date that she had started, her age, and her benefits.

Quality Review staffers, an organization that "grades" schools on performance and growth, visited the school and met with staff in late January. Notice of warnings were sent to each educator.

For the first time, the school atmosphere grades were declining.

Ms. Johnson took nothing into account in her words and actions. Instead, she blamed her staff for not "welcoming" her because she was the boss and not them. She actually demanded that teachers arrange grade conference calls on Sunday nights, calls that she would tape and be a part of.

Decent adults and long – term professionals felt helpless. The more they complained to the union, the more they realized that they were speaking to deaf ears. It was the same with the DOE. After all, many people thought teachers were getting paid well more than their worth, that the majority were pedophiles, and that they retired at young ages; teachers became millionaires, some thought, on taxpayer money.

Teachers found it hard to teach. They were too busy reading multiple letters in files that never should have been written. They were forced to attend lunch and prep meetings and were given reading and writing assignments Ms. Johnson actually graded and kept in a secret set of files she kept locked to all.

Ms. Johnson "surprised" classrooms with walk – through evaluations. Every teacher was bombarded with letters for their file and nasty vocal remarks. Her motto became "Teachers have to accommodate parents at all costs." She ended each written document with this quote.

Ms. Johnson refused to have a social committee, and thought that staff members were there to teach and not be friends. "Teachers can't be friends with aides, aides can't be friends with parents. Parents shouldn't want to talk to me, unless it is an issue their child, and then it better be a good issue," she would blurt out over and over to anyone who she thought would listen.

If you asked Ms. Johnson, she would brag to the other administrators how she has her staff "in tow" and how she had them afraid of her. Behind her back, they knew how the teachers were thinking and how parents were starting to send their families to other schools.

Teachers in Tier I kept quiet. They had a few more years and knew they could not afford to be fired. They got their salaries and benefits and believed in the union. They were taught from a young age, and in their homes, that unions protect their workers. Remember the Triangle Factory Fire? It would have never have happened with if unions had been around.

So, quietly, a few staff members took the steps to visit their representatives in the Queens and City offices and e-mailed top officials, including then Union President Randi Weingarten. Despite some cordial words and promises of "looking into" the issues, along with handshakes and union – printed pamphlets of how to deal with harassing principals, nothing was done.

It was clear in the documentation that the union could not bring any charges against the CSA or administration union members. They could have administrators change schools or fire them. All the teachers could do was to gather information.

This went on for about eight months.

CHAPTER 14

Ellyn was suffering both physically and psychologically. She was hurt in the crossfire of a fight, as food that was thrown in the hallway had landed on her right ankle. Ellyn received multiple letters in her file, including a record of taking off for her mammogram an hour early, which she had never done before, and the secretary tried to dock her pay. Contractually, she was entitled to the time, and when the principal received a call from the Queens UFT district office about this, she retaliated with a letter, claiming something about "taking advantage of a new boss." Ellyn also found herself the victim of false claims of verbal abuse and corporal punishment on four different occasions, all based on Ms. Johnson's accusations. In each case, there were no complaints, no evidence, and no witnesses, nor required paperwork documented by the principal. Yet Ellyn was found guilty of corporal punishment for not calling a parent about a trip issue on a Sunday night after 10 p.m., despite the various questionable tactics that arrived at this conclusion.

Actually, four staff members were in the same situation, which seemed odd, since in the entire fifty plus years of the school's existence not one staff member had come close to such accusations, much less investigations and filed reports, all coincidentally involving the principal as initiator, witness, and detective.

For the first time, Ellyn and Michael were arguing. They raised their voices, slammed doors, and cancelled plans. Nothing serious, but it was enough for both of them to realize that work frustrations were taking a toll.

The school year ended, and Ellyn got an unsatisfactory rating; for the first time on her annual review, there were comments by the principal. In fact, the entire staff received negative comments. By this time, the rest of the administration hid their faces, and the union was nowhere to be found.

Parents came to the defense of the staff, writing multiple letters and making phone calls both anonymously and in volunteering their names and contact information for follow ups. Yet, nobody received a call, a letter, e-mail, or any kind of communication.

That summer, Ellyn and Michael decided to take a vacation to Italy during the first week of July. They actually went for 11 days, giving them enough time to return for visiting day. Ellyn arranged for any food, presents, and any of her children's requests to be bought, delivered, and sent directly to the camp itself. Money was not an issue. Her sanity was the issue, and well as bringing "romance" to a new level with Michael. They were still having sex, but without the creativity and longevity that they once were experiencing.

Italy was wonderful. They stayed in Capri and were beach front nearly their entire trip. They walked the sand, read books, drank bellinis, nibbled fruits and anti – pastas and dipped breads in various flavored olive oils all day.

They talked, spoke, and whispered, held hands, leaned on each other's shoulders, and giggled the day away.

They also spoke a lot about Ellyn's situation at work. For the first time, Ellyn considered leaving, walking away from all the hard work, the expenses for her education, her pride in all of accomplishments, and her potential income, insurance benefits, and pension.

They even discussed buying a timeshare in Mexico and the possibility of Ellyn contacting some of her past business connections and being self – employed in a marketing consulting business.

Michael and Ellyn made love on the beach, in a bathroom, in a motel restroom, by a food vendor stand, and in the hotel room – over and over again.

They came home refreshed, more in love than ever before. Ellyn's head was cleansed. On the plane ride home, they held hands and spoke endlessly about the upcoming visit to camp and anticipated only the most exciting time watching the girls swim and play tennis and Michael putting on the golf course with their son.

Upon their return, they opened they garage door and led the driver to the entranceway, where their luggage was left. Their housekeeper was home, watching television in her room with her significant other. They had gone shopping, stocked up their pantries with groceries, cleaned out the pool, swept the patio and BBQ areas and made sure everything was in working condition upon Ellyn and Michael's return.

The next day, a Monday, Ellyn realized that she had been planning her class reunion, as she had done every year. However, with Ms. Johnson, she could not take any chances. She felt sad for the parents and her students. Several of them had left her messages while she was away with a similar theme. Where could they transfer their students to?

Ellyn was sad. These were some of the school's best families. Some of the parents had attended the school themselves, and their own mothers had been active in the PTA and in the local library, church, and community organization.

The next day, Ellyn received an unusual letter in the mail. There was no return address. In the envelope was a copy of a news article. A student from their school, apparently a sixth grader, a recent transfer out of their school, was arrested for bringing a bag of drugs to his camp. A flood of calls, e-mails, and texts followed among the staff. Apparently, what was not discussed in the article was that drugs were found on her in Ellyn's school, which many found out about in what was reported in the media. Ms. Johnson actually found the drugs falling out of her pocket as she was following her in the hallway one morning. She was not alone. She was with the dean, a 20 – year veteran staff member of the school.

"No response," was what the UFT leaders told staff to say when asked. "Many of you don't know what really happened anyway, and none of you ever filled out online incident reports, student concern reports ... get the idea???"

Somehow, news spread that the dean transferred to the new lottery school a few blocks away with no explanation. Most did not know what he did or did not know. Everyone questioned the move and Ms. Johnson' involvement in the entire case. Rumors surfaced that, in addition to the drugs, the student was being sexually abused and emotionally neglected and that child services were brought in to remove the girl from the neighborhood permanently after she finished her community services as part of her sentence.

This child had been selling drugs in and around the school.

It was the first week of August. Michael and Ellyn were preparing for their children's return from camp and a visit with their parents in Florida.

Ellyn was making flight arrangements to return early, as Michael reminded her of what they discussed in Italy. She hesitated, but decided to listen to Michael and stay with her family.

She confirmed that she fulfilled all of the required UFT contractual obligations, which they followed up with formal documentation stating Ellyn did not have to go in before the city – mandated professional development days. She also questioned her rating. They told her not to worry because she could grieve it, but with her reputation, tenure, and since this was her first and only U rating, she could look forward to a better school year.

They even said "off the record" that things were going to change without detailing any specifics.

Enough was enough. Several other teachers were not going in, either. Last summer proved nothing, and they were expecting another winter of Hell.

CHAPTER 15

Melissa was trying to become a good teacher, "A better teacher," was her motto. In reality, she was a good teacher, but in her mind, she could do more, become highly effective; there was always a room for more, more improvement and dedication.

But within her life, her surroundings outside of her school building, life went on without Melissa, and to that, she turned a blind eye.

Melissa lost touch with almost everyone in her life; people from her home, community, college, and even acquaintances that she was starting to socialize with from her jobs, teaching courses, and local hangouts.

Melissa had nearly given up on dating. She began to talk herself into thinking she was ugly, too smart, too busy … any excuse to build her self – esteem.

Many within Melissa's age range were getting married, including the new co – workers at her school, even those who were not as pretty nor as focused on their careers as she was. Since she was an only child, the exception to several miscarriages after her birth, Melissa grew up with nine first cousins who treated her like a sibling. They were also within a decade of ages, and even without the obligatory holiday gatherings, cousins on both sides of her family supported her through birthdays, camp visits, prom, and simply hanging out. Three of her cousins were among those whom she considered to be her closest of friends.

Those relationships were changing as well, as each was developing into their own adulthood, with careers and marriages; two were moving out – of – state. One cousin was gay, and even he was involved in a serious relationship, with thoughts of living together and adopting a child in the not – so – distant future.

Behind her back, her family was getting concerned. Her aunts and uncles did not know how to broach the subject with her parents. But after the latest gathering, at Melissa's parents' home with over forty people on Thanksgiving, they all felt that enough was enough, and that her parents, if not her, needed some sort of intervention.

Melissa was actually rude at her family's Thanksgiving gathering that year. She made excuses not to help when it was time to serve or clean. She kept cutting off conversations and redirecting them to her. Actually, she would direct them to her school: the greatest lessons that she taught, personal information about her students and their families, the extra seminars that she was volunteering for; it kept going on and on and on. If someone tried to ask her about something else, even if they simply asked if she had seen a movie that was recently released, or caught up on the newest Faye Kellerman novel, she blew it off and went right back to how great a teacher she was.

When everyone left, each other household commented on Melissa's behavior and how she treated them, especially her parents.

Two aunts treated Melissa's mother to lunch to discuss the issue. Unknown to them, Melissa's parents were well aware of her behavior and the change in personality and had concerns of their own. They were also arguing, which seemed routine with Melissa about her current state.

Her parents had seen a psychologist a few times, and with no resolution, ended the sessions and decided to look the other way and not lose their only child.

Melissa reacted by calling and coming home less often and starting arguments without merit. She made excuses to miss family gatherings, screened her calls, and did not return messages. On several occasions, cousins would offer to fix her up, and there was always an excuse that was an obvious lie. She claimed to be dating someone, or was simply too busy to get involved.

Her thirtieth birthday was coming up fast. Melissa was doing well at her school; however, she was starting to see a pattern of conflicts with several staff members. She talked herself into a state of confusion, thinking that her concerns were simply jealousy. To her credit, Melissa's lessons were good, even great, and she did have the support of her students, their families, and her administrators. She was always the staff member chosen to represent the school at functions and meetings after hours, and on weekends. Many staff members with other responsibilities were relieved she could relieve them of an administrator's pressure.

Melissa had her routine: wake up, go to work, come home, do more work, order in food, work until she fell asleep. She went to sleep, many times, with her laptop on her legs resting in bed, using the television as background entertainment.

As her birthday approached, there was much debate over whether or not the family should plan a celebration. When Melissa accidentally found out, she immediately tore into her parents about how they were so inconsiderate of her and asserted she would never show up.

Her cousin called her and invited her to dinner alone, with just her, her husband, and Melissa. Melissa invented an excuse that her friends were taking her out.

In reality, Melissa grabbed two slices of pizza from the corner takeout. On her way home, she nearly tripped on a stray cat. Promptly, Melissa picked up her furry new acquaintance and they shared pepperoni, two beers, and a quart of chocolate chip ice cream.

This eating was not helping her figure. The once – athletic Melissa had gained ten pounds that she was having a difficult time losing. She cut her hair into a pixie cut; while it made managing it less time consuming, in reality, the cut did not highlight Melissa's best features. She stopped shopping, and while looking professional, her clothes were starting to show their age. She stopped doing manicures, pedicures, and body massages. She always told herself that she had no time.

The following week at work, her assistant principal, Terry McNulty, wished her a special birthday, and the social committee bought cake and drinks from Costco to sing during that month's required staff meeting. Several co – workers who were feeling sorry for her chipped in for a gift certificate to Macy's, and parents and students brought in cards, chocolates, and bouquet of flowers.

This was Melissa's life.

CHAPTER 16

The following Friday afternoon, students were dismissed and Melissa went back into her classroom. As on most Fridays, Melissa stayed until 5ish preparing lessons and reorganizing desks to fit the differentiated lessons that she was preparing for Monday. She worked on her group boards and updated her library, making sure to level it so that each book was accurately labeled by the codes used through Teacher's University curriculum guide, as mandated by her school, in ascending order. She also bought duplicate books to divide by subjects. Melissa bought reusable book bags for students to exchange daily and for Melissa to leave notes daily in each bag for each student.

Every night, Melissa sent a class newsletter via her class Google account. In addition, she wrote personal notes to each family at the end of each newsletter. She also sent copies of each of these notes to each administrator.

All these extra hours, effort, and the money spent on supplies were often the qualities ignored and even purposely misconstrued by the media like the Bloomberg administration, former chancellors Joel Klein and Michelle Rhee and all the other critics. They claim that teachers work only 6 – 7 hours per day, take off weekends and summers, and walk away young enough to get a sizable pension and a second career with potential for another lucrative retirement deal.

Yet, most teachers did these "extras" not for recognition, but because they considered it part of their obligation to their profession. Melissa, however, took it to an extreme. For Melissa, it became an obsession.

She was about to leave, and as per school safety regulations, she had to sign out at the main office and confirm the time that she was leaving.

As usual, she was the last teacher to leave, with only the principal and some custodial staff circulating around the building.

Without warning, Terry McNulty walked up behind her and tapped her shoulder as Melissa held the pen in her hand, finishing her signature. Melissa and this assistant principal, Terry McNulty, had been friendly, shared lunches, and they would occasionally meet on weekends for lunch or dinner. Terry had been a transport from a Midwestern school. They had a lot in common, both being single, alone, and seemingly uninterested in the outside world.

Terry started small talk with Melissa regarding the busy day. Supervisors from the regional offices had made a surprise visit, and there was a potential fire down the block by a small store, which meant dismissal would have to be altered for buses and parent pickups. These last – minute events caused extra work for the two assistant principals.

"Do you want to grab a quick glass of wine with me?" Terry continued.

Melissa gladly agreed. They met 15 minutes later by a bar within walking distance from the school. Coincidentally, as they were about to sit by the bar, Juan, one of the custodians at the school, walked in. As Terry waved him over, it seemed a bit odd to Melissa, but being Juan was a friend to all, she quickly ended her train of thought. Melissa was glad to be out and did not mention her suspicions. Besides, Terry was one of her supervisors, and Juan was always helpful when she needed supplies and extra cleaning for her room.

They stayed, gossiped, ate, and drank several shots. Melissa was starting to feel tipsy. She looked at her watch, and feeling queasy, excused herself to the ladies' room. She returned and paid her part of the bill; before she left, they agreed to do the same the following Friday, as long as no one else found out about their dinner. Gossip often gets twisted, and it was nobody's business.

"So glad we are friends," Melissa said to Juan one day at school. She liked the feeling that two people actually cared for her.

The week flew by. As planned, all three met promptly at 7 on Friday at the same place. They giggled and gossiped about some of the kids and the mothers that complained constantly about really nothing. Terry confided that two of the teachers would not be asked back next year and that two gave noticed of retiring in June. Really, she should have never mentioned it, and she swore them to secrecy.

Melissa was getting tired; they had had more than the previous Friday. They were really enjoying themselves, or so it seemed. It was almost 11. Melissa mentioned that she had to go. Juan told her not to worry, that he would drive her home and offered Terry a drive as well. Here and now, they were equals; there were no superiors, no competitors. It was a meeting with three friends. Juan suggested that they do this every Friday night, which got no response – but, also, no rejections.

They decided to stay and order more, actually much more; they asked for a bottle of tequila. The waitress informed the owner, who made his way to the table and suggested having some coffee and dessert on the house – and leaving. They had enough alcohol for the evening.

They enjoyed the cheesecake and coffee sent to the table, paid the check, and Juan told the women to wait under the awning. While in the car, Melissa noticed that Juan was driving in the opposite direction, actually back toward the school, and she mentioned it.

"Didn't Terry tell you she forgot something? She has to pick it up," Juan responded, and parked while Terry felt the bottom of her handbag for her keys. Juan told her that he would open up for her and proceeded to open his door. "Melissa, come in, it's late and cold out here," he insisted and then continued, "Terry would be upset that you are sitting in a car."

Terry went into her office while Melissa sat and waited for Terry. Juan walked in a few minutes later. Terry suddenly screamed, as if she slipped, so both ran into her office. Some books had fallen off the top shelf and it seemed as if they were aiming for her head. She swiftly moved away, barely missing some books and a vase that smashed into thousands of pieces.

Juan went to his supply closet and then went to the security area to make sure the cameras were off and alarms not on, since technically, they were not supposed to be in the building after 11 on a Friday night.

Luckily, not too much time had lapsed since they entered the building, so the alarms had not triggered.

Melissa did her part in cleaning up by gathering towels and some sanitizer.

On his way back to the office, Juan approached Melissa in the bathroom, looking in the mirror, rubbing her eyes, as if they had tears.

"What's wrong?" Juan asked with a tone of sincerity that caught Melissa off guard. She admitted that she was lonely and drunk. Juan put his arm around her shoulder, pulled his cart with the materials that he needed to clean the mess, and they proceeded to Terry's office.

Terry gave Juan a look that Melissa did not see. Within seconds, Juan had thrown a light dustcover over Terry's desk and leaned Melissa's body back onto the desk. He started kissing her, and Melissa, dazed and in a fog, was too weak to fight; in her drunken daze, she could not physically resist. Juan was able to get her back on the desk.

"What took so long?" Terry whispered to Juan, knowing Melissa had passed out. Terry started undressing herself. She joined Juan in sucking Melissa's breasts. Terry stroked his back, removing his shirt, and then unzipping his pants. Melissa was no longer aware what was going on. Juan kept entering Melissa, performing oral sex, and enjoying each other as well. Terry caressed and licked every part of Melissa's body Juan was not engaged with.

This went on for over an hour until both Juan and Terry realized that they had to get out of the building. They carefully woke Melissa. She questioned them about what had happened, for which they concocted a story. Melissa was embarrassed, yet somewhat happy not to be alone, to be included – although she would not admit it, even if she did not know what actually they had done.

They went their own ways the rest of the weekend.

Juan parked his car. He walked up the three flights to as he usually did, thinking to himself how he had to get his mother out of this building. She needed a lower floor and an elevator at her age.

Juan's mother cleaned homes to take care of her own five boys. His dad, who died earlier that year, drove taxis and worked in various stores so that they could provide a better life for their family than what they left as teenagers. Their hard work paid off: five boys with high school degrees, union jobs, benefits and many grandchildren.

In Spanish, Juan greeted his mama as he opened the door and she was preparing a glass of tea.

It was one of the few times they were actually alone. Juan made himself a plate of his favorite carne and beans and looked directly at his mother.

"Such a good decent boy, so hard working, so devoted."

Mama' kept saying that in Spanish and repeating it over and over – as if to say she knew something, Juan began to think uncomfortably.

"Mama', what would you do, a friend of mine at work is in trouble." Juan was leaning towards her and she reached out to him, rubbing his hands, wrists, wanting to grab and cuddle him as she did so many times as a boy.

Juan started talking, in a whisper, as if he were sharing a secret. "Mama', mi amiga muy trouble ..."

"Juan you are a smart boy, you have a good heart, you heart is filled with love, you do what you must, but remember ... Papa and I taught you good values. Your papa was put in positions all the time ... and some not always good, but in the end, he had to teach you and your brothers, and he is looking down on you now – "

"Yes, Mama'," Juan interrupted, "but this may be something bad, and my friend – "

"No, my smart boy, you must listen to me now," Juan's mother was emphatic, "what others do or say, friend or not, remember, Papa is watching you. Papa is watching you!"

"Sí, Mamá," Juan agreed reluctantly, "lo sé, I know."

CHAPTER 17

M elissa was dressing for school Monday morning when memories of Friday night suddenly made her sway her head and shoulders. She was starting to get glimpses in her mind and fluttered her eyes. Was it a dream or was it real?

Juan saw Melissa first, cleaning up during lunch. He said hello to her, then to another teacher, as if nothing happened. She took a breath of relief. Terry walked into her classroom later that day, checking on a student's status regarding his attendance for guidance. There seemed to be some discrepancies between the mother's notes and the counselor's. Terry gave comments to the class about how lovely they looked, walked around with her notebook, jotted down some of her own remarks, which remained private, winked at Melissa as she did to most teachers, giving her a sign of confidence, and left.

Terry spoke with Juan that Wednesday about Friday night. Both agreed to keep things as usual with Melissa, but keep it dinner, less drinks and an early ending. No sex. No manipulating Melissa.

Terry simply happened by Melissa's classroom door during dismissal. "Stop by my office before you leave," Terry requested. Melissa seemed worried. Upon arrival, Terry welcomed her in, closed the door and asked Melissa to handle a meeting the following morning with a perturbed parent. She handed Melissa some paperwork regarding the student, then as Melissa got up from her chair, Terry casually reminded her about tomorrow night. Melissa felt relief, as if everything was ok.

On Friday night, Terry made an excuse about being in school extra early for Saturday Academy, a tutoring program. Juan did not offer to take anyone home, so Melissa excused herself and walked to the nearest subway station.

During the next few weeks, everything appeared natural. Terry formally observed Melissa, and gave her a satisfactory report, with several commendations and only one area to improve. During that time, and under the UFT contract guidelines, Melissa technically got the best report that she could have gotten. A teacher received either a satisfactory or an unsatisfactory rating.

For Melissa, she had no worries. Besides, she even socialized with her leaders. At this point of her life, she had more contact with them than with her family members, even her parents.

Things were going in a copacetic fashion, day after day. Melissa seemed happy, and her students were her family. She had to cancel the next two dinners even though she really didn't want to. She did have to meet her parents for birthday dinners. They even drove into the city, which they rarely did, trying to accommodate Melissa and avoid any conflict.

During one of her reading small group lessons, seemingly out of nowhere, Melissa started to feel nauseous – maybe, she thought, from some bad tuna she had for lunch. She thought nothing of it and did not want to sidetrack the students from their thoughts. Five minutes later, she felt a pang and had the sourest taste in her mouth. She knew that she had to leave. Luckily, her room had a bathroom attached, so she opened her class door, waved to the security guard, who was her friend, and made motions like charades to get to her immediately: She was about to vomit.

She made it in time to vomit in the toilet without leaving a mess. Her students, who loved and respected her, sat quietly and watched, except for one little boy that made jokes and got out of his seat. The security guard scared him enough for his commotion to stop.

Melissa made it back to her group, finished this lesson and proceeded to write something on the board for the next subject; instead, she didn't finish her first sentence. She fainted.

9 – 1 – 1 was called immediately, and it proved to be too much excitement for this school. Everyone was scared and concerned. Melissa rarely got sick; those at school either loved her or resented her, but no one wished her ill.

In the emergency room, Melissa awoke, and several tests were given. Questions were asked about what she had eaten, drunk, whether she took any drugs or medications, allergies … and to several, they already figured out the answer. They had seen this so many times before.

Doctors asked about emergency contacts, immediate family members, to which Melissa requested no contact.

As this was going on, the principal was filling out the government – mandated incident report, with information to the best of her knowledge, not aware of her assistant's nor favorite custodian's friendship with Melissa. Melissa acted as professionally as she could, thinking she had a sudden attack of a stomach flu.

The truth was quickly leaked to the staff "anonymously." However, people were smart enough to keep the gossip outside of the school and away from Melissa.

Melissa was pregnant. She took herself home, against the hospital's staff advice. She was in a fog, angry and shocked.

Terry and Juan met in a diner outside in Astoria. No one would know them there.

"Terry, I understand, we have fun, and it has nothing to do with school." Juan was troubled, Terry could tell, but she couldn't know what was really behind his fretfulness.

"What if she talks," Terry pushed the subject. "Does anyone really befriend her?"

"Not to my knowledge," Juan replied, and then "Maybe we should help her some way, you think?"

"What are you thinking, Juan," Terry responded curtly. "We have to be careful, remember? I need her next September."

Their conversation ended, but Terry could still see that Juan's mind was elsewhere.

Soon afterward, Melissa was called for her post – observation conference. In the meeting room, she found Ms. McNulty dressed very formally and tapping a folder.

"Terry, good to see you," Melissa began.

"Ms. Dobbs, please sit."

"So formal."

"We are conducting an official meeting; this is your contractual required post – observation conference."

Melissa gave her a look of confusion as Ms. McNulty began scuffling papers and finding her formal report.

She handed Melissa a copy. As all teachers do, she looked at the very last page by "Remarks" to make sure she received a satisfactory remark.

"Melissa, you certainly know how to prepare a lesson," Terry began. They went down the list of notes – objectives, standards, materials, differentiated lessons, small groups, leveled readings – all a part of a good lesson.

"When you questioned the little boy, Zack," Ms. McNulty commented, "he started to cry. Is he afraid of you?"

"No, he is afraid of answering the wrong information and having the others make fun of him."

"Is that why you used the puppets for him to relate to?"

"Yes, he found his comfort zone in the theater groupings and relates facts to felt."

"Very clever."

Melissa looked at the bottom page where recommendations are listed. For the first time, Melissa had five suggestions.

"What's this?" Melissa asked, somewhat confused. "You suggested some more questions about the main character since you wrote you never heard any? Didn't you read my observation? Hear the responses?"

"Melissa, you are my best teacher, but my superiors are watching my every move. Every teacher needs more criticisms."

"I know you did the work," Terry continued, "but I can't have anyone question as to why I don't give you some professional development."

Melissa felt confused by the contradictions, but she felt she could not oppose Ms. McNulty's assessment in light of their shared secret experiences.

CHAPTER 18

Mark and Sarah were celebrating their fifth wedding anniversary as if it were their wedding night. However, this year was different; Sarah thought that she was pregnant. She told no one, since she had miscarried last year, early enough for others not even to recognize the change in her body, but still an emotional experience and enough for her and Mark to be saddened by the loss.

She did not tell Mark. Mark was so unsuspecting that she decided to keep this secret just a bit longer, enough for her carry the baby longer than the last one and without changes in her behavior and body.

The "picture perfect" couple was well on its way to becoming the "picture perfect family." There was no way that it could not be: all beautiful, outgoing, giving to others, and interesting.

The afternoon after their celebratory dinner and theater night out, Mark and Sarah went back to their jobs. That day was a meeting of the weekly program that Mark had founded and helped with. However, now there was a hired staff director, Richard Smith, paid through the Department of Education. Others would not volunteer as Mark had when people were getting paid for the job. Mark was different.

Many felt Mark's attention should have been focused on his other businesses, for they were growing. Nobody could initiate and follow up the deals like Mark, despite full – time employees in his father's office trying their hardest. Mark received professional satisfaction when helping children in need, despite all his business achievements. By working with his family and building his own contacts, he made everyone around him happy.

Several times, unofficial warnings came from co – workers and friends at the "United Federation of Teachers" that if something went wrong, because the volunteer program was on "his time," he could one day see himself in an awkward situation. Each other staff member was hired through the director, and nobody else had worked at the school or was a certified teacher. If there was any kind of accident, or incident, Mark was on his own, because contractually, teachers were not "covered" for arrivals, dismissals, preparation times, lunch duty, and after – school and weekend programs.

Mark, aware of his reputation among his school environment, blew off anything related to getting any kind of trouble and laughed it off as a joke when mentioned.

Richard Smith ran several programs under the titles of early childhood summer camp, after school, weekend, and individual tutoring. He was not an educator. Smith had never studied for an education degree. His background was actually in sales, working from store to store and always being fired to a multitude of reasons. He was able to obtain this position as a fluke. Smith was at the right place at the right time, and by sharing several handshakes, the job was his. He was a friendly guy, with lots of connections to money within the education and business communities where the programs ran. In each location, for each program, he made it seem as if he was running the program, but in reality, he used his charm to make sure that one or two staff people ran the show while he took the credit. He was so charming that they did not realize how manipulating he was. He knew what he was doing, yet he would give nice gifts, invite them to privy political parties, and introduce them as valuable assets to community leaders.

He always smiled and thanked people endlessly. While not always at a location, he made sure to show his face enough so that the impression he was always there.

Parents loved these programs, and would pay large amounts of money that they did not have to ensure their children would have a safe place to stay with supervision while they were working. Some of the programs included cultural activities, trips to museums, and theater performances, some of which these kids would never have experienced. While these programs were supposedly subsidized, parents often said, they were still costly, to which they got answers that the programs and staff cost lots more than they had thought. Being as busy as they were, nobody investigated further.

One afternoon, as students were finishing the final moments of that day, Smith passed by the room Mark had been working in, walked in and made complimentary comments to the group of six. He reminded them to take all their belongings and thanked them as usual for coming. Two third grade boys ran over and gave him a tight hug, pulling on his suit jacket and pants. That was Smith's strength, "making everyone feel special." As he was walking out the door, he turned around and casually mentioned to Mark, "As always, great job, do me a favor and make sure to see me before you leave."

Mark followed Smith to his desk, where Smith proceeded to hand Mark a pile of papers and folders. "Do me a favor, review these – you are the best person for this, and with your expertise, it should take no time and show perfect results." Smith knew Mark would never refuse, and Mark knew Smith appreciated it. After all, Smith offered to bring a dinner receipt to him to be reimbursed for his efforts over the weekend.

Before Mark could change his mind, and just to be polite, Smith said something about thanking his wife for sharing him on his free time. "How's she doing," Smith questioned, not really interested, just to "play the game." Mark responded, "Just as beautiful and special as ever."

The next day Mark was sitting in the teacher's lounge during his preparation period when the union rep walked in and handed out notes about changes in the copying protocol. "What is this?" one of the veteran teachers asked.

"Even when you produce and pay for your copies," the union rep explained, "you need three approvals, one from the teacher – grade leader and two from your next – level supervisors."

"It makes no sense," claimed another teacher.

"It's my money," voiced another.

Mark turned to his six colleagues and commented with disgust, "I'm calling the union office."

In a quick response, the senior woman teacher said, "Mark, just go along and keep quiet. You know what happens."

Mark responded, "What happens? You can't get fired."

"But your life will become miserable. Teacher after teacher who challenges a principal somehow gets letters in their file, additional work, public ridicule and eventually people stay away from them."

Another teacher chimed in, "Mark, don't, you are young teacher and a good one, and the students really relate to you."

Mark looked at the union rep, "Won't the union help me? Aren't there rules to these things?"

"It's not so easy; principals all over the city are taking advantage of seasoned teachers, who valued their seniority status for "perks.". Teachers started having meetings during lunch and after – school, setting up e-mail accounts and have separate cell phones for work – related use, for which they paid with their own funds. Despite violations to union contracts, principals suddenly demanded more access, more accountability for things like being able to help nurse a student and help with home issues that were not school – related ... you get the picture."

Chapter 19

"Melissa, I need a big favor." Alex Donovan, Melissa's DOE friend, said when he called her. He needed help with a family member. The young student had a history of poor grades and behavior.

"I need a special boy to have a special teacher. He likes attention and needs the kind of focusing that you can give him. He has tremendous potential, but given his current class situation, can't seem to do his best."

"Send his records," Melissa responded, "and I'll review them."

The next day Melissa received a hand – delivered package. She took it home and studied it carefully while nibbling on her salad and half – eaten sandwich.

"Seems ok, can't understand Alex's concern," Melissa spoke out loud to herself.

The student's public record contained medical updates, some academic notes and two documents about school changes.

What Melissa did not know was that the notes on previous behavior issues, academic failings, summer schools attendance or lack of it, and pertinent documentation had been removed. School records are often incomplete, for many reasons. Many people have access to them, and many people are required by law to update documentation and include outside paperwork. Because no one is really trained on how to complete a file, and files are often tampered with so that social promotions, grade changes and school transfers are often the "wrong" information, student file numbers and records for academics within any Department of Education system are confusing and should not be deemed as reliable sources.

Alex Donovan was intentionally misleading Melissa Dobbs.

The following day during her preparation period, Melissa volunteered to meet Terry McNulty to discuss her new student.

"I hear he is a lovely boy, and I am looking forward to working with him," Melissa commented. McNulty, knowing the truth about why Alex Donovan's relative was really being admitted to the school gave Melissa a confusing look. She heard about the child from a conversation with the boy's previous school administration.

"Ok, whatever you say, but remember, whatever happens with him, it's in your hands. I don't need any problems on my school's records. I plan on getting an 'A' on our school grade and nothing less."

Melissa didn't understand McNulty's concerns. She blew it off, stood up, reached out her hand to say good bye, and left McNulty's office, feeling confident she was helping her friend, Alex.

Coincidentally, Alex Donovan was assigned to oversee Ellyn's administration. It turned out that he had supported Ms. Johnson. Ellyn had heard about him from Melissa. However, it seemed as if Melissa did not know the real Alex Donovan since many staff members and parents were finding out little "details" about Mr. Donovan that seemed "unprofessional."

The following September was hell for Ellyn and her co – workers. The union sent several representatives to their building and conducted several meetings about procedures, filing grievances, and responding to several of the complaints submitted against Principal Johnson.

While all this was going on, Ms. Johnson ignored all the signs around her that she was failing her own bosses. Classes were smaller, more regulations regarding safety and curriculum were being violated, and all she felt that all she could do was retaliate. Tenured teachers like Ellyn were getting verbal and informal complaints, letters in their file, and unsatisfactory ratings, with criticisms regarding the district required programs that Ms. Johnson had little to no background on. When once asked to model lessons by the union representative in front of the entire staff, Ms. Johnson walked out angry.

The next morning, a veteran teacher was called into the principal's office in a closed – door meeting that, until this day nobody has heard what was said and done. However, it was the last time that any teacher or representative had ever voiced conflict with any of the administration in that school building.

Ellyn had an observation, written up as a formal, with an unsatisfactory rating. Ms. Johnson was so clever on how to write these evaluations up that she found a strategy that worked so that no teacher could ever fight her and win.

Ms. Johnson had a layout of several observation reports she used for staff evaluations at home. To individualize each to make them sound unique, she would change names of students and write on little bits of actual lessons. Her remarks were similar, just changed enough so no one would be able to tie them together.

She complained about groupings, supplies, or one or two students being neglected; she included everything that could seem plausible and with no factual evidence nor witnesses. This was a precaution that was followed just in case a union grievance should ever take place in front of "impartial" judges and people outside of the building.

By the holiday break, Ellyn had received another such evaluation in writing. This time, she actually organized a meeting among staff and senior union representatives that was to remain private and confidential.

Apparently, one of those attendees went to the principal and told her everything that went on and highlighted that Ellyn organized the assemblage of attendees.

Michael and Ellyn planned a ski trip for the family during Christmas week vacation. They returned the day of New Year's Eve. They purposely arranged it so that Ellyn would have time to rest before returning to work.

Michael kept reminding Ellyn what she said over the summer about quitting. "Whatever happened to the calls you made about working on your own?" Michael would question, knowing the answer was that Ellyn had never followed up.

Ellyn did not have to worry about returning to school; she had received formal papers in the mail that day. They were papers for an investigation. Ellyn was not to report or make contact with anyone from the building.

She was to report to the human resources department of the Department of Education, where she would meet the supervisor who would be in charge of reassigning her during a pending investigation.

CHAPTER 20

Terry thought that she recognized a parent. She saw Juan entering the lot, but avoided looking until she was sure that the coast was clear – no people, no cars, no students hanging out either waiting for pickups or just "hanging out" with the temptations of causing a commotion.

Juan also kept his eye out, wearing a baseball cap and oversized eyewear. He even borrowed an overcoat and scarf, so if someone thought they recognized him, the different outerwear that he always wore would confuse them enough to have them think it was someone else.

He opened Terry's car door and swiftly closed the door and put on his seat belt. Terry drove, in fact sped, out of the adjoining lot to the building next door to the school. The school's lot was too noticeable and discernible, if someone should see them.

They were the only two who knew the truth. They knew, and so did Melissa, but Melissa was in no condition to tell anyone what happened. As of yet, Melissa had not spoken, but would she talk? It was still new. Melissa had taken some time off, and when in school, stayed alone, knowing people were talking all sorts of "accurate details." Melissa got pregnant by a married staff member, some said, and others said by a parent or an old boyfriend, and she was planning on getting married.

They drove over the tunnel, to a secluded diner off a highway in New Jersey. They sat in the last booth by the kitchen, which smelled from all the grease within the stovetop crevasses and ovens. Nobody in their right mind would be running into them here. They ordered coffee, and realizing that they had to talk and could not do this often, decided on multi – course dinner specials.

They first questioned if the baby was conceived that night. They were throwing ideas around for a few minutes, knowing full well that Melissa had no friends and no men in her life, much less any kind of sexual involvement.

Their concerns for Melissa were only about three minutes long. Both admitted that they had no contact with her outside of work and even on school premises, avoided her.

Were their actions and names traceable?

How could they be sure Melissa would not talk?

Were there any witnesses or any evidence that they could possibly confiscate?

How far would they have to go in order to protect themselves?

They sat for three hours, barely eating, which their waitress noticed and commented on. "Would you like to try something else?" They politely declined.

Terry told Juan that in no terms were they to have contact except for business, and for that it should be minimal, cleaning forms, supplies and tasks. But, Terry added, not to make it obvious, such as asking others to do his work or asking staff to speak with her when he could clearly get the job done himself. If he was assigned to clean her office, still do it.

"Try not to talk with me on DOE phones, no e-mails, or any other traceable communications. We also must try to avoid eye contact and signals," Terry demanded.

They both agreed that they needed a concrete plan, the sooner the better, in case Melissa decided to talk.

Juan said it simply: "What if we tell the truth?"

"Are you suggesting what I think you are?" Terry questioned him, knowing that she could never afford to go the way Juan was suggesting, but in fact that something more dramatic in another way might be necessary.

This was no easy matter, they needed to think – and quickly. They paid their individual bills and finalized a meeting in three days at the restaurant across the street, but this time taking separate vehicles.

Between the times that they met, they had responsibilities and bosses to answer to. Luckily, little had anything to do with Melissa. In fact, Melissa had taken several days off.

The principal sent Terry to the district office for some professional development with several other assistants from the area. Since she did not have to report back to her home base school, she arranged to meet one of her cousins, a lawyer.

They were close, and by signing a consultation agreement, Terry was insured that their conversations would remain confidential under attorney and client privileges. Terry told him the story, leaving out small tidbits, and referenced the main characters as "people she knew."

Her cousin told her, in no uncertain words, to "cut the crap and listen." Terry was potentially in deep trouble, far beyond school regulations. If the Board of Education felt the need, they could bring trespassing charges against her alone, which would lead to a biased hearing and termination.

She needed to open up and tell the entire truth, or she could walk out. She did eventually tell the entire story, from beginning to end, even tearing up as she mentioned the step – by – step group sex that they forced upon Melissa.

"Do you realize some would construe this as a rape?" Her cousin slightly questioned. He then told her they had to remove Melissa from the building.

They had one advantage in the entire situation: Melissa had a reputation. While known as a brilliant teacher, many questioned her emotional stability. They had her family background that would help them prove their point.

They worked together on a scheme that seemed plausible. The lawyer asked Terry if she was sure that Juan was "on board." She assured her cousin that he was.

Terry and Juan met. She told him her plan. "It's brilliant, simply brilliant," she assured Juan, and both went their separate ways, knowing their parts in the plot, and Terry breathed a sigh of relief, not knowing that Juan drove straight from that meeting to tell his mother once again of his concerns for "a friend."

Melissa, a blossoming teacher with at least another twenty years of educating ahead of her, went along each day with a cloud over her head. She felt nothing for the baby and questioned keeping it.

Her only happiness was teaching: contact with her students, the many awards that she had hanging both at home and in school that she would now glance at more than usual.

Her family kept trying to call her, but she left their messages unanswered. Her parents suggested she move home and take a leave, which made her feel offended, and she blew them off as well.

She received a call from the PTA president; they were still planning on rewarding her at their annual June appreciation luncheon as their "teacher of the year." Her personal affairs were none of their business, she was told. They appreciated what she did for their children.

And that remark was correct. She initiated and got the school grants. She made contacts with educational vendors that gave the school all sorts of perks for their association. She excelled in all her evaluations and started thinking about administration courses.

She even maintained her contacts in TWEED, from all her extra jobs.

Who would go after Melissa Dobbs? Not the New York City Board of Education, of course.

CHAPTER 21

Meanwhile, Terry instructed Juan to get an order of protection against Melissa. They both knew that eventually Melissa would try and confront both of them Terry, being her supervisor, was the least likely choice.

He would need some evidence of Melissa pursuing him. He had some texts on his phone that he could edit to make it sound as if she were making plans that he did not want.

Terry would have to do some dirty work of her own. She would also have to figure out ways to get the principal behind her. The principal would be a hard sell. Things had to be done so that, by the time the principal was involved, her hands would be tied.

Melissa walked into work as if nothing was different. She signed in and saw her principal, who greeted her with a formal "Hello."

It was Monday morning. Melissa came to work. She decided to stay focused on her classroom, her lessons, and on doing the best job possible. She was still early enough in her pregnancy so that it was not noticeable to those who were not aware of the situation. Her doctors told her all was going well and her health was good. She took all their advice and tried to think in terms of being a mother, but questioned whether or not she would be able to be a mother.

Melissa also knew that eventually she would have to speak with Juan.

McNulty was out of the building at a professional development session in Manhattan.

Juan saw Melissa and called Terry. Terry couldn't talk but warned him to avoid Melissa – unless – he saw a chance to have a pubic confrontation with Melissa and build up any evidence and if possible, gather witnesses.

"Brilliant," Juan said, adding, "They'll think she's nuts . . , most already do."

McNulty reminded Juan to think before he acted; after all, Melissa could ask him for something as simple as cleaning up a mess from a child, or fixing the heating in the classroom in a professional manner that all staff did routinely.

However, they had to get Melissa to instigate contact that could be conceived as questionable.

Little did they know that over the weekend, Melissa rehearsed at home how to keep her composure, what she was going to say, and how she was suggesting several resolutions to the problem when confronting Juan. After all, she thought, Juan was her friend, and he would help her out.

Melissa was tired and hungry. However, she stayed to prepare her class for the next day's lessons. Time flew, and before she knew it, it was almost 6. She proceeded to her sign out book in the main office, followed procedures, and then remembered she had left a book in her room. Juan was in her classroom, sweeping the floor with his back towards her. Within minutes, there were screams from the classroom, loud enough for anyone on the floor, maybe even on others could here, if they were still working in their classrooms. Juan positioned himself to where the security video monitors could clearly see them together, without actually being able to hear the conversation. Within minutes, Melissa left in tears, and Juan had all that he needed.

Juan went directly to the police for an order of protection. He game them copy a copy of a letter he was going to personally hand deliver to the principal, the superintendent, his union representatives, and to the offices of the legal department of the NYCDOE, telling his "version" of how Melissa was "treating" him.

Juan accused Melissa of physically attacking him, pursuing him for months, and falsely claiming that he was her baby's father. He claimed that he never wanted to hurt Melissa, and up until now, for the sake of the school, had ignored all of Melissa's advances.

Terry had actually written this letter. It was a brilliant move, already written, knowing that Melissa would confront him sooner or later.

To make matters worse for Melissa, Juan actually had cut himself on a nail while with Melissa and turned the story into something about Melissa scratching him in a fit of rage.

Melissa got a certified letter to report to the TWEED office downtown. She did not have a clue as to why.

She called the principal, who was supportive and sympathetic, but stated that the situation is out of her hands and now in being investigated by the Board of Education. She wished her luck and told her not to contact her anymore.

Melissa now had to wait, in more ways than one.

CHAPTER 22

Mark couldn't believe his eyes; the words and numbers in the reports he'd been asked to read didn't make any sense.

Could his eyes be teasing him? Thinking he had copies of earlier paperwork, he walked into his bedroom, opened a file cabinet drawer, and sure enough, he found what he suspected: different numbers and labels by programs.

Maybe the paperwork was filled with mistakes. He tried to call Smith and left several messages with no response.

His last message was "Hi. It's Mark. I think you accidentally handed me some paperwork that you need to review. Good thing you gave me it before you handed it in to the DOE. Your numbers show you are personally profiting from monies that belong to the school and to this particular program. Call me when you get a chance, Again, this is Mark, I hope to hear from you soon."

Mark and Sarah went out for dinner, as they did every Friday night. Sarah had wanted to go to the movies. The new Tom Cruise movie opened with great reviews, and Mark also wanted to see it. They were planning on it, until Mark broke the news over cappuccino and tiramisu that he had gotten some unexpected paperwork, and since most of the weekend was filled with work and two parties, he had to complete it tonight. But he would make it up to her afterward.

Mark sat by his desk and reviewed the first set of paperwork. He added his notes with sticky notes and highlighters. He jotted down some ideas, which he made copies of, and from what he saw, all looked fine. He then proceeded to read some more, and as he was engrossed in a packet, his elbow knocked over a pile of folders. He got off his chair and kneeled to pick up the piles, trying to keep all in the order in which it was given.

He was pushing papers together when he saw something that seemed out of place, something that did not fit in the realm of the program that he was working on. It was marked in red, with a warning of privacy on it.

Mark stopped reading the other work. He became intrigued. Apparently, this packet was misplaced. Some of the ideas, wording, and facts seemed to make sense. This set of papers discussed the program that Mark was working in. The introduction, goals, and business statements all made sense, with few errors. However, the budget paperwork was all out of sync. Something was not adding up, and this was especially true for the claims of payment for staff, supply costs, and outcome success numbers.

Mark got upset. It was a mistake. Something was not right. These papers were not for his eyes and were put here by accident. Mark wondered why, because, after all, Smith was a nice guy. He went to get a drink, something strong. Sarah had called him to join her in the bedroom. "Honey, you promised," Sarah complained, but sex was the last thing on Mark's mind. He shrugged her off. Sarah finally fell asleep, and Mark could not think of anything but what he had just read.

Mark had a good business sense, yet was starting to suspect that something was going on that seemed like a scheme for someone to profit off of money dedicated to the program. Maybe Smith was an innocent victim of someone trying to scam him. Mark thought about it, and although he did not want to admit it, he faced the fact: Smith was involved in something illegal, and because Mark had seen the information, he could be in trouble, too.

Mark knew that he had to play dumb and finish the work that Smith asked him to review. He jotted some more notes and made copies of everything, including the paperwork that he was not supposed to see.

He went to the gym, tried to focus on his personal business, and went with Sarah to their friend's 30th birthday party. He was quieter than usual and could not share with Sarah anything about what he read, which he really did not like, as they shared everything.

Meanwhile, Smith was at his own home on Sunday when he listened to Mark's message and he realized he made a major mistake. He had given Mark the wrong papers, the bundle of documents that could incriminate him. What was he to do? He could not admit to Mark that he knew anything was wrong.

Smith saw Mark that Monday briefly, and they smiled at one another as they usually did. Neither mentioned anything.

Wednesday, after the tutoring program, Mark gave Smith the package of papers back to him. Smith acted grateful for all the help. Mark said nothing, making Smith wonder if maybe Mark didn't figure out what was really going on.

Mark accidentally left a sticky note on one of "those" papers. Smith had his answer. He knew who he had to call and what had to be done.

The next week, Mark was called into the principal's office over the loudspeaker. In the office were all the administration and a process server with a package of papers.

"Mr. Ollins, you have been served."

CHAPTER 23

Mark knew that he needed someone to confide in outside the school system. He called his college roommate and close friend, Benjamin Bronstein. Bronstein could never understand Mark's career choices, for he thought Mark could have had success on Wall Street or in a top law firm. Mark was the only one of their clique that did not pursue a six – figure career.

Most of the guys drifted from Mark because of his career choice. They couldn't relate to his hours, union support and the content of his conversations, since so much included their work environments.

Benjamin was different. He loved Mark like a brother, and both were groomsmen in the other's wedding party, and organizers for Mexican bachelor parties. Benjamin's wife and Sarah were close friends, too.

Benjamin's specialty was corporate tax law. He was pursued and rewarded with a spot at Wilzig, Nahon & Connor, one of the top law firms in the country, with offices on each coast and in Washington, D.C.

Mark swore Benjamin to secrecy, even from their wives, which in turn was promised. They sat at a corner table at the newest steakhouse midtown, and quickly ordered scotches – straight.

They went through detail after detail. Mark and Benjamin both jotted down notes. Benjamin knew little about this area of law, but knew others that he could ask for advice.

Mark told Benjamin that he was going to meet with NYSUT attorneys, who would work on the case pro – bono. Benjamin mentioned, "Before you make any decisions, don't talk, just listen, and don't make any decisions before you consult with several people, different attorneys, different people from the union and private legal firms."

NYSUT, or the New York State Union of Teachers, was a union group, and thus, its attorneys had a reputation of being 9 – 5 workers and seemed like "puppets pulled by the strings of their bosses." While they were representing educators that were evaluated for success in the classroom, attorneys here received a paycheck regardless of their success rate in court or hearings.

Benjamin mentioned, "You have no choice but to go to your union first, and many attorneys will ask you if you contacted the union staff and their reaction to your case."

Mark listened, but really did not understand what Benjamin was saying. "Mark, research teachers online that blog and how the media covers their cases. Many of them went first to the NYSUT legal teams, lost their cases, and then went to private firms."

"How do you know that?" questioned Mark.

"I read the local papers, pictures all the time of teachers walking to their cars, by their homes ...I guess even their board of education identification photos, if that is where the sources are."

"Wow"

"Enough years of collecting discovery for cases ... and winning," Benjamin laughed as he tried to assure his pal that he had to be careful and mindful of how he talks and interacts with everyone now.

"I am sharing with you," Benjamin continued, "be prepared for the worst – case scenario, then be pleasantly surprised with any positive outcomes. I'm with you all the way."

They actually enjoyed their visit, and after salads, surf and turf, and amazing onion blossoms, they realized the time, said their goodbyes, and reassured each other that they would be in touch shortly, and that all their meetings were confidential.

Mark was to report to TWEED Human Resources for his reassignment. He entered the building on Broadway, admiring the old architecture and old – fashioned elevators. As pretty as they were, two were also broken, so instead of waiting for the only working one, he walked up to the third floor and saw a long line standing in front of one room. He stood on line for almost an hour until he was finally called in.

About a dozen teachers were sitting, two were sleeping, and another was eating a smelly sandwich. A woman was crying. Mark went to sit next to her. "Hi, I'm Mark, are you OK?" She looked up, happy someone came to listen.

"I can't believe this. I'm teaching over thirty years, the most senior teacher in my school. A parent called the principal and said that I yelled at her daughter and touched her inappropriately. The girl insisted on hugging me after I rewarded her with a sticker for being the only student to answer a question correctly. I called the student's dad and did not know the parents were going through a rough divorce. The mother told the principal I acted unprofessionally, and the student admitted I hugged her when she got up in front of the class. Next thing I know, the mom's attorney threatened the principal about future contact with the father and a lawsuit."

The room got busier as the day progressed.

Another woman that he met was eating all over her shirt, sipping coffee loudly, and spoke in a rasp, rude tone. When he did not hear one of her questions, her reply was sarcastic about him being there because he could not hear. Upon completion, she asked him to remain outside in the hallway and not to leave the building. Although he had not realized it, this was going to be the rest of the morning, until another woman advised the fifty or so people waiting that it was now noon and they had an hour for lunch. "Please sign this sheet, along with a cell phone contact so that if you are late, we can trace your whereabouts."

Mark sat there until a 3 p.m. dismissal. It seemed odd that the union agreed that days spent in investigation periods were longer than those in actual classroom time. However, they were. Mark was told to return for another day, and sat there for entire week, until Friday afternoon, shortly before 2 p.m. At this time, he was told that he would have to go to the district reassignment center and was told to meet his supervisor in his office Monday morning at 8 a.m. He was given a metal pass to use as his sign in/sign out monitor and signed several papers before he left for the day.

"Mark Ollins, please come in."

The DOE staff member had a filthy, disorganized office stacked with loads of papers, folders and empty Styrofoam containers smelling with leftover food. "Mr. Ollins," the staffer began, "are you aware that you cannot go near your school while you are awaiting a full investigation? Are you aware that you will be paid, attendance will be recorded, and you are to follow all the instructions of your immediate supervisor in the location you are about to be placed?" Mark could not believe this slovenly person had so much control over his professional future.

"I see you work in Manhattan," the staffer continued.

"I also live there."

"Too bad, maybe you'll think about your actions if you ever get back to your job. You'll learn to travel a little."

CHAPTER 24

Ellyn had undergone a similar experience only a week before. She too was told to meet at a center in Bayside, Queens. She was told that there would be about fifty teachers there, scattered throughout floors and from different schools. She was told not to discuss her case, especially since many in the building worked directly with her supervisors and knew many of the other teachers in the building. The irony was, that although she should not talk, it did not stop almost every DOE staff member immediately from calling all their contacts within her school and in this building to gossip as to why Ellyn was there in the first place. Some knew Ellyn, and some had even worked with Ellyn on various projects and seminars.

On her first day, two teachers asked if she wanted to join them for lunch. However, they told her that they were driving to a local diner and would not be back for at least an hour and a half. This violated Ellyn's 45 minute lunch allowance, and she politely declined. It was for the best, avoiding awkward conversation.

Ellyn's first day was in no uncertain terms, boring. She was asked to make copies for about ten minutes, and for the rest of the day, she sat at a desk and did crossword puzzles.

Unbeknownst to Ellyn, only a few flights up, in a small office filled with overstuffed metal cabinets and piles of dust, sat an uncomfortable Melissa. People on her floor knew her well and left her alone. She asked the custodial staff several times to help her with the dust situation and told them how the dust could hurt the baby when breathing it in. The first two times, they smiled at her as if they cared and would take care of it. The third time, the custodian grew angry and responded loudly so everyone could hear him on the floor, "You're a crooked teacher, clean it yourself, you should be fired, not here wasting money."

She went to the ladies room and cried in a stool. After five minutes of crying, her supervisor walked in and yelled at her for not sitting by her desk. They were docking five minutes off her lunch.

CHAPTER 25

Because Ellyn, Mark, and Melissa were all tenured teachers involved in investigations and 3020a Education Law cases, they were human experiments in the teacher termination system.

While the mayor claimed "rubber rooms" ended, this was far from the truth. People were assigned locations to stay and do no work for extended periods of time. If they were given assignments, they were simple, like collating, stapling, or making copies. They were assigned jobs that people on minimum wage or interns would succeed at for free. Despite all the computers, they were not allowed to use them, and depending on where you were or who supervised you, you could not use the staff refrigerators, ovens, or eat when others ate in the public space.

Within buildings, there was always a trust issue, even among those under investigation. Principals, aides, in fact any school staff could and would be placed in a situation like this while undergoing investigations. Safety officials, school crossing guards and bus drivers were sitting throughout the five boroughs waiting to hear if they were going to be fired.

The negotiations between the UFT and the Mayor were supposed to produce better quality teachers, and fire those with legitimate issues sooner and cheaper, but that had not been a result as yet.

Mark was asked to set up two breakfasts during his first week. Both hot and cold food was served, including smoked fish, sausages, bacon, and chocolate chip pancakes. He was politely asked to leave without being offered as much as a cup of coffee. He was then asked to clean up the mess, pack up all the extras, and only then offered cold, picked at, unappetizing food and beverages.

Ellyn decided to take up crocheting, and took it to work every day. She decided to knit quilts for her guest rooms; and most simply left her alone. One day, she was asked to listen in on a meeting and hand out the various papers as needed. She realized half way through the program why she was asked. Except for the name change, she had been a participant in the same professional development the previous two years. Not only that, she was the assigned turn – around staff member to have mentored others. Now, she was witnessing this while handing out papers. When it was the question and answer part of the seminar, a question was asked of the moderator, who instead of answering it, raised her hand and gestured to Ellyn to respond. She then introduced Ellyn in a polite manner, not as a reassigned teacher, but as a colleague who volunteered to help out. Ellyn gave the response that was hoped for, then sat in the back corner until the end.

Afterward, Ellyn walked over to the moderator and thanked her for the opportunity to participate and for treating her with respect.

As with most teachers under investigation, Mark, Melissa, and Ellyn found that many of their co – workers, even those considered friends that shared so many personal occasions together, suddenly found themselves "unavailable."

Administrators knew who was close to whom and shared all this with investigators and attorneys. Union representatives warned staff to avoid discussions, interactions, and controversies involving those being investigated. Indirect threats were made to those thinking of helping the accused, especially if the principal wanted to get rid of them.

Some called to gossip, some called to see if they could actually get on the good side of the administration and then relay all the information that they got confidentially against the accused. Some administrators initiated contact with staff to find out what they knew, as well as their own opinions and possible actions.

Two weeks into the reassignment, Ellyn parked her car by the usual spot that she found daily, grabbed a cup of coffee at a local cafe, and proceeded to take her badge out of her pocketbook, when she noticed someone sort of familiar. She could not place exactly who it was or where they had met before, but that they definitely knew each other, and not from this building. Mark proceeded up the stairs before Ellyn got close enough to catch a closer look.

Two days later, during lunch break, a man was on his cell phone while trying to grab a quick bite of his sandwich, and he was trying to handle too much. He was waiting for the elevator when as he turned, he bumped right into the right hand of Ellyn, and spilled her container of black hot coffee all over her hand and coat. It actually had hurt.

He apologized profusely, neither recognizing the other. She was trying to clean herself off. Others around them handed them tissues. Someone set the custodial bell for a clean – up. They were too busy making sure Ellyn's hand was not burned, and cleaning off her coat. It took a few minutes for the commotion to end and for them finally to look at each other eye to eye. Ellyn spoke first, "Wait, I know you, but from where?" Mark thought a moment, then responded with several answers: grading groups of city tests, professional developments, places that were work related.

Ellyn at first thought, maybe, then squinted as if in deep thought. "No, where did you grow up?" They proceeded into the next available elevator gradually questioning one another and getting engrossed in conversations. They finally figured it out – New York University.

Ellyn couldn't believe her eyes. "Mark, is that you?"

"Oh my God, Ellyn – – it has to be a decade, what are you doing here?

Ellyn didn't quite know what to say.

"Mark, if I recall, you went into your family business."

They exchanged cell phone numbers and texted each other throughout the morning, those texts revealing the systemic failures in the treatment of these dedicated teachers.

"LOL, can't believe we are both here."

"What are you doing?"

"Rather be teaching."

"Wait, I got a job, stapling together some dittos to be handed out to principals."

"Can do that and text, and get paid."

They did not get into personal details while within a DOE surrounding.

"Ellyn, be honest ... do you have a hard time talking about all this ... I mean, the accusations, the responses from all around you. How do you deal with it?"

"Michael is my biggest support, he listens, he thinks and he couldn't care less if I left this and stayed home."

"Sarah would be there for me too, however, she has a full load, and truthfully, I want her to lean on me."

"Marriage is a partnership ... does anyone know how you feel?

"This whole experience just makes my parents say, 'See, you should have just stayed with the family businesses all along, who needs that crap, with parents and kids who don't even appreciate you?'"

"In some way, they are right. I am amazed how my co – workers, parents who leaned on me to help their children and even some of my former students have shunned me."

"Sarah and I are trying to have a baby ... and the last thing on my mind is bringing an innocent child into this mess."

"Don't ever think you did anything wrong ... whatever you decide to do and discuss with others, you are a decent person and are being used as a pawn in a dirty game."

"Thanks – those words have meaning, especially from someone who can relate."

They met during lunch the next day by the Chinese takeout. Ellyn usually brought her lunch, but was getting tired of the "dirty looks" surrounding her and did not have to take it during her free time as well. She never ate a big lunch and stuck to a simple egg drop soup. Mark was following his protein regime, ordering steamed shrimp and vegetables with no rice and no extras.

Mark confessed that he had a few concerns about his case. As close as he was to Sarah, she politely gave him his space. His parents offered to hire the best attorney that money could buy, and use their business media contacts to help him garner public support. He graciously declined.

Ellyn laughed, because she was going through the same feelings and reactions. Michael reminded her over and over again about how she mentioned she would quit, and he too offered all of his money and connections to screw over the school system. Before this situation, Ellyn could easily quit, but now she was stuck. If she quit, she would be required to take the settlement agreements that the union and Department of Education agreed upon, and she could never again teach within the city system. Ellyn would have to admit some guilt, which she refused, and most important and most damaging to any person who settles – she could never sue the Board of Education. Given that history has proven that more facts come out after the fact, and within statutes of limitations, she could never consent to any settlement of that nature. Papers had to be signed and filed, which made many details public, and in this day and age where everyone uses Google, you never know where this information could damage Ellyn or Michael.

A month had passed, and for Ellyn, she decided that she had to let her life go on. She planned a family dinner, inviting her brother's family and Michael's divorced sister and her two children over for a dinner and to watch her daughter's soccer game afterward.

Mark, on the other hand, started therapy sessions, under the advice of Benjamin.

CHAPTER 26

Wayne Gray, Esquire, was a well – known attorney with a small office in lower Manhattan. Wayne was born to immigrant parents, Holocaust survivors, who lost everything in the war. They were both the sole survivors in their immediate families. They lived on the same street in Hungary, both from large families with parents that were monetarily successful and religious. They were both taken in separate roundups to Auschwitz, and as orphans, came to the United States. They were both in their late teens. They married so that they would stay together, and eventually fell in love after all the years of suffering. They were determined to build "the American dream." They thanked God every day for their ability to survive Hitler and his atrocities.

When Wayne was a baby, a distant cousin on his father's side made contact with the family. Unknown to Wayne's dad, this father had a brother that relocated to New York years before the war, and despite efforts because the timing was too late, had tried to buy him passports. Before the cousin died, he made his son promise to find their family, if any survived, and as promised in the death – bed wish, he would one day visit the Gray home. He gave them money, but more importantly, he gave them jobs within his own business, as well as names and addresses of people who could help them.

They had each other, their four children, all named for their parents, and a knot in their stomachs that hurt so much that the only medicine was success. They worked many hours, and helped the business expand so much that money came in, especially in the early 1960s. However, they knew what it was likely to fall into a comfort zone of money and security. They lived as if they had little, and stressed education and hard work to their children as the only path to success.

While many of Wayne's friends enjoyed the activities in summer camps and family vacations, he held two summer jobs. Many of his friends went to private, even far away campus colleges, while Wayne's only choice was to go to Brooklyn College, live at home, get a part time job and work toward an advanced degree. He resented his family deeply at that point of his life. However, as he graduated Summa Cum Laude from New York University Law and was offered a job at a top three firm, he realized what got him there.

Wayne started his own law firm three years later and never looked back. He had a reputation as being aggressive, and found success taking on clients who never seemed to have a chance and winning their cases. He also hated discrimination of any kind, given how his family was treated, so with some intense strategizing, hard work and meeting success case after case, he made a "boutique" out of discrimination and employment law. Few lawyers practiced in that area at the time, outcomes were not guaranteed, and respondents often did not have enough proof or money to finance their cases.

While Wayne was selective, he also thrived on the "underdog."

During the following decades, Wayne's firm grew, and his success became news, winning several multimillion dollar verdicts against Fortune 500 companies. But he never forgot where he came from, and expanded his original offices to two floors in the original building that he opened his first office in.

Despite offers to join larger firms with million – dollar salaries and large company benefits, Wayne stayed true to what his parents instilled in him. He did not make it as hard on his children, giving them all life could offer, and when the time came, all three joined the firm.

That knot in his stomach was always pulled tight.

CHAPTER 27

A month had passed and both Ellyn and Mark had heard nothing from the union offices. After the initial contact and after receiving the documentation, a form letter was sent to every accused staff person about getting in contact with the union attorneys directly.

They ate lunch together daily. Their talks were about family, memories of college, and everything but the positions they were in. It was the unspoken bond. While both cherished their marriages and valued the trusts on their friendships, both spoke little to their respective spouses about the renewed reunion.

Mark did not tell Ellyn, but he did take Benjamin's advice and spoke with a professional. He went to a psychologist recommended by one of Benjamin's colleagues whose patients were undertaking the difficulties of harassment in the workplace. She had a reputation of being unbiased, even when making thousands helping a patient and getting paid for testimony.

The psychologist recommended that Mark start seeing her routinely, or as timely as he thought that he could visit. She also suggested that Mark continue his exercise and diet routines and try to figure out how he could talk about his suffering in more detail.

Mark found the exercise and diet easy to follow, but talking and rehashing the facts, not to easy.

While Ellyn sat day after day letting time slip between her fingers and allowing the Board of Education time to embellish more lies into their "mock" investigation, Michael took action behind the scenes.

Michael had confided in one of his corporate attorneys. They wanted his growing business and contacts, and Michael knew that they would do nothing to jeopardize it, including giving him wrong advice. He contacted Wayne Gray.

He met them in person, and without Ellyn's knowledge, shared the documentation Ellyn received about the charges and the laws regarding Education Law 3020a. He also brought the paperwork, even though it was just a formatted letter, because he thought that he should cover all bases. Michael was hooked.

Convincing Ellyn to meet Wayne was going to be hard.

He had no choice. After the kids were fed and involved in homework, Michael told Ellyn that they had to talk, privately and no with interruptions.

He took her to his study and shut the door.

Michael admitted everything: taking the paperwork, the meeting, his thoughts, and his concerns. He did not trust the union: why hadn't anything been done? He could not understand why Ellyn was under the impression that this was all going to end soon. She was given assurances from her school representative and from a call with the Queens representative. "The City is so far behind with investigating and litigating these cases that it could take a year." She was told that it was to her advantage, being that it is extremely hard to prove these cases, much less ever fire a teacher. "That's why the public hates us."

Ellyn's record was perfect, and her witness statements and history of the school all played in her favor. Most importantly, there was no evidence against her.

Over the next two days, Ellyn made several unreturned phone calls to several people within both the UFT and NYSUT.

Then, she had Michael call Wayne Gray and make an appointment.

She did not mention anything to Mark, nor anyone else.

Within a day, Michael got a text to call Wayne Gray, with his office and cell phone numbers, and a name that referred them. Wayne was expecting his call today.

Michael made an appointment to meet him two days later, after a court appearance and Michael's round of patients. Ellyn took off the Wednesday that they had reserved for their first appointment. Michael rearranged his schedule, and they decided to make a day in the city. Their appointment was at 9:30, Wednesday morning. Michael surprised Ellyn with orchestra seats to The Book of Mormon, the hottest Broadway theater ticket, and booked lunch at Orso on Theater Row.

Ellyn brought an attaché case full of papers that she thought were prevalent to the case. Ellyn made copies of everything, what she thought was her complete file, documents regarding the school, staff meetings and union notes given out to the entire staff, and articles about teachers in investigations. She brought one of the many "logs" that the union suggested each teacher keep in case they were ever questioned about parent contacts, administration issues, and as a backup for themselves.

Wayne was impressed with Ellyn's professionalism, although as Michael's wife, was not completely surprised. Wayne also knew, while this case would probably be a contingency fee payment, Michael had the finances to back any major expenses needed for investigation and hiring professionals, something few union members have as support. This was a case that Wayne wanted to take for many reasons. He knew just from the two – hour meeting that Ellyn was innocent, a victim, and most importantly, he would win, which would have limitless benefits.

Gray's office was impressive; professional, yet not too intimidating to his type of client. In the waiting room were many articles in frames hanging on almost all of the space, along with several awards. Several journals had labeled him "A Teacher's Best Friend" and "The Union's Worst Enemy" since he won suits for clients fighting most of the unions, government agencies, and major corporations. He was always the "David" that fought Goliath.

When he was sure he understood Ellyn's situation, Wayne was very detailed about what they could expect.

"Here's the deal," he explained. "Once a teacher undergoes an investigation, chances are they will never teach again. Individuals are usually stressed out and do not have the funds to fight the government, period."

Michael had to interrupt Wayne:

"I don't get it – Ellyn is a fine, upstanding individual and a damn good teacher. Those kids she teaches – they don't get the attention from their parents the way Ellyn pampers them."

Ellyn chimed in, "I don't just teach, I nurse, mother, sister, buy them supplies, respond to their calls and e-mail for them all hours of every day and night, regarding any requests ... and believe me, many of them ask for help that goes way beyond explaining a classroom lesson."

Wayne interrupted with "Ellyn, unfortunately, you are not the exception, you are the professional that most educators are."

Michael insisted, "Money is not an issue, Ellyn's reputation and quite honestly, her pension and retirement is at stake. She didn't spend all that money getting degrees, hours depriving our own children and many years of successful teaching to be harassed unfairly and lose everything she has worked so hard for."

Michael noticed all the wall hangings of Wayne's media and awards.

"You certainly seem to have experience in these types of cases."

Wayne stated, "I can have you call any of these clients for a referral. They will tell you what comes with a case like this"

Ellyn questioned, "What does that mean?"

Wayne answered, "Please listen carefully. There are no guarantees about any outcome. Most people end up settling because they are put to their limits. My success is based on choosing to represent clients that I believe in and in turn they believe in me."

"What does that mean?" Michael said, looking confused.

"It means I don't always win, and many times people don't get what they want in terms of settlements, but it means that many, and I have a good percentage above average on my record, people get what they want in terms of legal wins, and second chances, and some get a good monetary settlement.'

"Remember, the government does not want the exposure of losing cases and giving away taxpayer money."

They spoke for about an hour. Michael was clearly impressed. This guy knew his stuff. They shook hands, agreed to speak again, and said their farewells.

As per Wayne's advice to Michael, he made sure everything at home stayed as normal as possible. He booked tickets to Florida for February, started working on a summer trip to Asia, and took some time off to attend more after school sports games that the children were playing in and school activities.

Before they left, Wayne brought in two associates to introduce them all, and to inform Michael and Ellyn that, if they proceeded with the case, they would be directly involved. It seemed as if everyone hit it off and said their goodbyes knowing they would be working together soon.

When Michael and Ellyn reached their car, they both looked at one another and knew exactly how each other felt. Ellyn just blurted out, "Call him back and tell him we'll send a retainer."

They spent a wonderful romantic day together. Michael had a knack for making Ellyn feel secure and temporarily forget about any trouble. They came home in time to order in some Chinese and sit together with their children. Ellyn was in such a good mood and she requested that dinner be set in the dining room, and on better china, not her best, but not the everyday pieces that had cracks or missing spots.

Later that night, they made love and both forgot that Ellyn had to return to the reassignment center the very next afternoon.

As she walked into the building the following day, she shared the elevator with a familiar face.

CHAPTER 28

Melissa was reassigned to the Queens center only after sitting for some time in a room alone in her school in the back of third – floor gym. Terry and Juan thought her isolation in the building would work to their advantage, since any kind of outburst would eventually lead to Melissa violating the orders of protection. They got a break when the union made arrangements for her to sit with other staff under investigation.

Melissa's parents went behind her back and got her reassigned to this location, wanting her far away from the school, the gossip, and Juan; they did not know about Terry at that point. They called one of Melissa's friends in the union and quietly changed Melissa's assignment.

Melissa gained some weight, but was getting used to her physical position. She left her home extra early to make sure she would arrive on time.

Melissa and Ellyn saw each other just outside the entrance door, under the awning.

They recognized each other immediately. "Melissa," Ellyn began, "you look exactly the same as you did in college."

"Ellyn, it's hard to believe it has been so long."

"Life has changed drastically for me, do you remember Michael? Well, we have been married over a decade, and we have two beautiful daughters. And you?"

"Still single, this teaching thing, it has taken up most of my life."

"I remember you having a cousin you were close with," Ellyn responded. "How is she?"

"Still the same – she's married, with children, and living the kind of life my parents want for me."

'You'll get it in time. Do you keep in touch with anyone?" Melissa asked.

"Nah, occasionally I get a school alumni update, but being single, and now with this ... who wants to?"

"Did you run into Mark Ollins? He is somewhere in this building."

"You must be kidding! Mark, didn't he go into real estate? I never saw him as a teacher; he came from such a rich and business – oriented family."

"Don't say anything if you see him. Act surprised he is here."

Ellyn gave Melissa her cell phone number and asked her to call soon to meet for lunch.

That morning Ellyn was given an assignment, one that took most of the morning, to clean out a closet. She was asked to work on a ladder and remove moldy, rusty materials on shelves that had not been touched in years. There were mounds of dust. This was against her contract, and it was clearly an unsafe situation. She called the Queens office and was told via message that she should just do it because she did not need any extra controversy against her.

Ellyn somehow went to the main custodial office and got some disposable gloves. The custodian mentioned in a somewhat jokingly manner that she could take some cleaner and scrub the shelves as well, but he was serious.

She tried talking to her supervisor, but to no avail. It was almost 10:00 and she had no choice; nobody was there to defend her. She went into the bathroom and called Wayne on her cell phone. He told her to document everything; her cell phone records would prove her calls to the union, and she should try to take pictures of the shelves before and after she completed the task.

He also told her that, if he was not available, to ask his receptionist to get in touch with his associate for an immediate response.

Mark finished his morning's "task" and figured he had over an hour before lunch to do "his thing." He started reading some of his paperwork, as he had no problems continuing his private business connected to selling goods with ties to his family business and his own investment portfolio, which had grown quickly into a successful mini – business advising others with small investments and developing nice commissions.

Ellyn, meanwhile, had completed about half the project when Mark texted her, inviting her for lunch and suggesting they meet in 10 minutes. She forgot to tell him about Melissa, but texted Melissa to get ready and wait by the parking lot entrance so the DOE staff wouldn't see them. It was nobody's business which teachers befriended other teachers. It was their time.

Mark came down last and was surprised that there were two ladies waiting for him. Ellyn apologized for not letting him know ahead of time that she had invited another teacher. Mark had wanted to be alone with Ellyn. He had wanted her advice on something. Oh well, there went that, he thought.

Mark recognized Melissa immediately. They actually had sat through two classes together and might have even have shared some notes and ideas. Realizing the connection, Mark quickly forgot about what he wanted to discuss with Ellyn and was happy to sympathize with someone else over their ongoing predicaments.

They sat in a corner booth by the Chinese again and ordered. Melissa ordered a lunch special, extra soup, and two drinks. Both Ellyn and Mark looked at each other in disbelief.

Melissa felt comfortable immediately and just started blurting out her entire situation. She would not let either Mark or Ellyn get a word in edgewise. Melissa bragged about her teaching skills as if Mark and Ellyn were inferior educators, to which both responded by remaining quiet and giving each other an eye signal.

She started with her school, how she was one of the most frequently recognized staff members, and how she had so many friends within her staff setting. Mark tried to question her about her parents, which she ignored. She went right back to talking about her close friends, Terry and Juan. She was eating as she was talking, not realizing how much she was consuming. But, as she mentioned Juan, her voice changed, she put down the plastic utensils, and the tone and sound of her words were softer and slower.

She told them that she was pregnant. Melissa did admit that Juan was avoiding her now. She neglected to tell them that he had gotten an order of protection against her. She also told them that she was confident that after seeing the baby, he would change his mind, do the right thing, and support the baby in a financial and emotional way. She was even hoping that they could build a relationship and marry, all for the sake of the baby.

They finished lunch and reported back to duty. Mark actually fell asleep, from boredom and doing nothing, until buzzing out at 3:00 p.m.

He went to the gym, came home, and went straight to his home office. He read several faxes, and then Sarah walked in from her day. Mark barely said hello while reading his paperwork. He did not kiss her and greet her, as was becoming the pattern since he received his investigation paperwork.

Sarah left him alone, but she was confused as well. Before this mess, they were trying to conceive a baby. With his growing anxiety, this seemed less probable. She did not know how much longer they would be able to handle this situation without professional help together. "Does any of this really matter – don't you want our baby?" Mark, realizing that Sarah would never understand, decided not to tell her he was seek professional counseling alone.

He also refused legal counsel outside the union. Mark was convinced that he would be supported by the union. He actually began using the time in Queens for his own work. He read papers, took notes, made some calls. Mark was lucky in that he sat alone all day in a computer room, and through one of the DOE tech people, he was able to connect to the internet on his own machines.

One day during lunch, Ellyn told the others that she actually got calls from both the New York Post and New York City Rubber Room Newsletter, since they had information that Wayne Gray was handling her case. Ellyn had made no comment to the newsletter callers and told them to speak to her lawyer, who also refused to comment.

The Board of Education also refused to comment, when coincidentally the very next day, the Post featured an article about a parent letter sent to the DOE – and ignored – regarding a principal calling parents "lazy asses" for picking up children late during dismissal. Several parents taped the incident and sent it to the press and to the heads of the various NYC Department of Education. The principal was Gloria Thomas, coincidentally,

Nancy's Johnson's best friend, cousin and principal in a school nearby. The press had pictures of them together,

Ellyn and Michael thought for sure that this would help her case, end her temporary situation. She would be able to get on with her life very shortly.

CHAPTER 29

M ark was the first to hear from the union. He made an appointment the following week with his appointed attorney. Coincidentally, Ellyn received a letter regarding her appointed NYSUT attorney. Again, these letters were form letters, just personalized with the appropriate names, personal information, and contacts.

Just as a courtesy call, Ellyn called and confirmed that she would not need the services of the union. When they questioned her about who she was using and what was going on in the case, she informed Wayne about the phone call, and he assured her she did the right thing; be polite, but not a fool. They were not doing anything to help her. Besides, he told her point blank, the union hardly ever wins, despite their claiming otherwise.

Wayne's strategy on Ellyn's case had changed a bit, since the press on the Johnson cousins. He told Michael to add security around Ellyn, possibly purchasing devices to help her in case she was "attacked" verbally, emotionally, and at worst case, physically. The DOE would not want any more attention on Johnson, and Ellyn's case could blow open a bucket of worms.

"Money is no object," Michael said. "Just get this horror over with." Wayne then reiterated to Michael that finishing this case, even with the best possible scenario, would take time, and few who were accused, if any, get off completely. Arbitrators are hired and paid for mostly by the days they work, many take their time to finalize decisions and make them public record.

"Wayne, that is not good enough for me, or Ellyn," Michael responded. "Hire anyone or purchase anything you need right now and get this done." Michael was not used to the words, no, can't, or won't. However, he recognized that he had to change his attitude. Court was out of his hands, and he had to remain strong for Ellyn and their three children.

The Marks family members each handled the stress of the situation differently. Michael and Ellyn did not share all the details of what was going on, but the children still feared the worst for their mother. They stayed away from friends whose parents would gossip and those that constantly would question them.

Their oldest, and most knowledgeable about the facts, seemed embarrassed that such ludicrous accusations were being thrown at their mother, and refused to bring friends home or talk to the younger siblings.

The youngest, who was old enough to know something was going on, but young enough not to understand, actually loved what was going on. When Ellyn came home, she had no lessons to plan, no work to grade, she did not look or feel as tired, and she was not complaining about her school.

And Ellyn, along with Mark and Melissa, was sitting along with every other teacher, aide, school security guard, and every level of administrator accused as they were, getting a full paycheck and benefits for months, even years. It was fair, after all, since some investigations never got even as far a hearing, for many accusations from angry parents ended unsubstantiated. The result, for the personnel so accused, was emotional distress, additional costs, time for travel, and the scars tied with being reassigned that would last a lifetime. Because Ellyn was not as tired as usual, or working at home as much, she joined a weekly canasta game and volunteered one night a month at the local community center to make and distribute food packages for those in need.

The next couple of weeks came and went without any major updates. Melissa took off one day to go to her doctor, and she talked a lot about Juan, with whom she had no contact. Mark went again to his therapist, and he seemed to be growing more anxious and was prescribed a minor sleeping pill.

One day, while they were having lunch alone, Mark told Ellyn about his therapy, He asked her not to tell Melissa about it. They knew that something was not right with Melissa and felt sorry for her.

Michael was being honored as Specialist of the Year by North Shore Long Island Hospital's Pediatric Division. He was recognized for the years of free work that he did for children with rare diseases or children with infections like AIDS, when others refused to care for them. The event was going to be black tie and held at the Old Brookville Country Club. Ellyn treated herself to a designer gown bought at Manhasset's Miracle Mile, and Michael bought a Ralph Lauren tuxedo.

Everyone in the family was looking forward to the night and to the pampering beforehand. Because of Ellyn and Michael's popularity, over 700 people donated money and attended the dinner, accumulating the largest amount of money ever raised for this hospital's event. Wayne bought a pair of tickets, something he usually did not do for his clients, but he knew that potential business sat throughout the ballroom.

Two retired teachers and close friends came with their spouses. Several teachers secretly gave small donations and asked that it be kept a secret, fearing Johnson and the DOE.

The night started out perfectly, and the weather held for pictures outside before the event. Everyone looked stunning. Both Michael's and Ellyn's parents flew up from Florida and almost of the extended family attended as well. The caterers outdid themselves, offering volcano martinis, with dry ice, baby lamb chops, and mini lagastinos, or lobsters on trays.

Not a thought of the troubles – they had, it seemed, not a worry in world.

Michael got up to make a brief speech and called upon "his better half" to join him by the podium for the presentation of his award. He was about to be handed a Baccarat vase with an engraving when suddenly a camera and a microphone came from out of nowhere.

People did not have a clue what was going on and thought that it was part of the program. A reporter started screaming something about the hypocrisy of Ellyn hurting children while Michael was being honored

"Isn't it true," a would – be interviewer shouted, "that you are going to be fired from the Board of Education for being incompetent?"

Michael grabbed the microphone and yelled, "That's enough." Wayne flew from his chair to grab Ellyn and get her out of there.

The secret was out: The night was ruined, and people were in shock the rest of the evening. Luckily, the result was plenty of video and witnesses at Wayne's disposal to use later on. Security quickly escorted the man out. While certain media had been invited to cover the event, one pushy education reporter misled the public relations coordinator in a way to sway her to let him in, telling her he was covering the event for a dental teaching human interest story he was freelancing, without mentioning his intent or outlet.

The rest of the night went on as planned, but very quietly. However, record contributions were received, which reflected on Michael and Ellyn, and the decor, food and music led most to have a delicious dinner, time with friends and an occasion to look their best.

The next day, Ellyn's picture was in the New York daily publication with an unflattering and factually incorrect article besides the photo: *"Incompetent Teacher Honored for Helping Children with Disease and Disability, Too Sick To Help Themselves."*

They met the next afternoon with Wayne Gray in his offices. His strategy had changed: two sides could play at that game.

CHAPTER 30

Mark was still waiting day after day for his union attorney to contact him regarding movement in his 3020a hearing. He thought that his case was different from other teachers and had his mind set on a quick and full vindication. Who wouldn't support someone in any profession that proved they could secure grant money, create and volunteer for a successful program?

However, the process was the same for every accused employee of the NYCDOE, regardless of teacher, administrator, or staff, especially if they chose to use their union's assigned legal team. Most did, since there were no out – of – pocket expenses except for thousands of dollars each paid in union dues annually to cover procedures costs. Typically, this was never fully explained to the person upon getting an initial paycheck.

Mark was loyal to the union. Benjamin also told him that the union should be the first place he attempt a legal resolution. After all, the union was large; it had changed safety rules and provided security with the power of numbers. It had money, a large staff, its own media outlets, and most importantly, political clout.

Still, growing gradually more worried with the slowness of the union in resolving his situation and with the inanity of his highly paid "make – work" duties, Mark began researching online blogs and even recent print publications by and about others caught up in the DOE processes.

The more he read, the more astonished – and disillusioned – he became.

Finally he called Benjamin.

He was blunt when he had Benjamin on the phone: "Man, I'm screwed. Teachers and more teachers are writing about how the union let them down even when the facts were on their side."

Benjamin responded, "Mark, it's a crap shoot; more and more people are getting disgusted with union antics, and teachers like those are a benefit to your case. Take notes, list names that you see over and over again."

"For what?"

"You will eventually will go to a private attorney, but at least now you can tell them you tried with the union," Benjamin explained, "Any private legal team will benefit from your business savvy. Most teachers are not in other successful businesses and have their family members sought out by important people, including politicians."

"I get it, thanks. And Benjamin, you'll see, I'll win – we may lose some battles, but we will win the war."

"Mark, you have a lot of battles ahead, so be prepared for unexpected attacks."

CHAPTER 31

The NYSUT offices are located in the main UFT building in lower Manhattan. It was easily accessible if one could get to it, by the Wall Street subway station; otherwise, the drive out of the city could make it a destination to hell. It felt like a world away from a classroom in the city. It looked more like a Wall Street Fortune 500 firm or a Top Ten International Branch of the Law Group; it was anything but an environment for people under 18, with the ability to comprehend adult life. It was minutes away from the buildings destroyed on September 11, 2001, and the location of the Triangle Fire Factory, which killed over one hundred people. Both were reminders of the history of New York, the history of the union, and their connection to education.

The NYSUT legal team was set up over several floors. They were the quietest offices that one could have been in, which was a dramatic contrast to the liveliness of a learning environment. They had easy access to when they wanted to take lunch, when they wanted a coffee or bathroom break, the use of copy machines, faxes, meeting rooms for large groups, and much better security than any school building. Attorneys and many senior staff members made very good salaries, without any kind of form of evaluating their success and failures on an individual basis. While the union boasts that they rarely allow a teacher to be fired, they can rarely boast total exoneration. Most teachers "settle" in order to leave, not sue, and get a satisfactory rating and recommendation to teach elsewhere, regardless of actual facts; this is often done to ease a budget or quiet a potential troublemaker.

The head of the legal counsel was situated in Albany, New York, and visited the offices routinely. Most of the legal team shared secretaries and interns. Office hours usually ran from 10:00 – 6:00. Teachers met briefly with attorneys once their case went on the record to pre – hearing conference dates. The lead time for preparation and communication between client and lawyer was minimal, and initial conferences were filled with standard questions about years of service, file materials, accolades, personal background, and offers of settlement, favoring the DOE to get rid of them.

Even NYSUT requests for discovery, the materials needed for defense work, were standard, and the information in a file was typically incomplete, inaccurate against their own contract regulations, and sometimes even tainted. The "claim" was that an arbitrator was specially picked by both the union and the Board of Education. However, even in media outlets such as the New York Post, arbitrators were mostly paid by the Board of Education and were afraid of Michael Bloomberg, not just for his clout of getting them jobs of education arbitration, but in regards to any arbitration jobs in other fields, particularly within government and unions areas. Both had large budgets to litigate a hearing before it got into actual state and federal courts.

Arbitrators loved these jobs. They, too, were their own boss, on the public's taxpaying dollars. They could charge over a thousand dollars a day with no accountability. Many of them rely on the taping of hearings and brief note – taking during the actual hearing while reading papers, text on cell phones, taking brief breaks for personal calls, and allowing their minds to wander everywhere but on listening to the facts for which they were being paid. Then, afterward, they could bill and claim hours of research and document drafting to produce a final verdict. Many of these arbitrators were paid lucrative salaries, but still complained that they were underpaid.

Many actually did complain, it became public knowledge in a lawsuit and publicized in the media that many arbitrators were not getting paid and left their positions with the New York City Department of Education.

CHAPTER 32

"Mark," Ellyn commented as they discussed their situations over another lunch, "Mark, you are young, smart, and talented, more than most teachers. And – you have backing to support you – a wife, parents who just happen to be wealthy, and an extended family people can't even define in a dictionary."

"Exactly what does that mean?" Mark was slow to see Ellyn's point.

"You know exactly what I am saying; don't play dumb. I say it again: You are a handsome, intelligent, personable man – every girl at NYU wanted you – and probably some still do when they read or see pictures of you with your family. It is time to get out of this shell, stop feeling sorry for yourself and get to work. You were never one to back away from working hard, don't stop now. It is as if God had a calling for you to stand out – "

"So, any suggestions?"

"First of all, talk to your wife – my biggest support is Michael – he wouldn't care if I said goodbye to all this and let him take care of me the rest of my life."

Mark chimed in, "Are you telling me that Sarah should support me?"

Ellyn chuckled, "Don't be Mr. Comedian – you know exactly what I mean. Talk with her, openly and honestly – your parents, too – especially your father. You should also go see a doctor and make sure your health is good. Take care of yourself, make sure your blood pressure and cholesterol are OK – you know, keep your body and mind in shape."

Mark responded, "You know I work out and watch my diet."

"That is a start, but emotional stress takes its toll on your physical being. Stay on top of it."

Mark broke in, "What if I don't want to?"

Ellyn looked directly at him as if she were about to punish a little boy who did something really, really bad, "Mark, stop living in a state of denial. For whatever reason, you are here. Face it like a man. I go home every day and have to face my children, my sick parents, take care of a home and stayed involved in a community. My husband is a professional who likes a wife to look good, stand by his side, and make him proud. Do you think this has been easy on me?"

Mark picked his head up, as if an epiphany had come into his path. His pupils opened, his eyes now alert.

"Stop feeling sorry for yourself, stop being in denial – Take a look at Melissa: She is not married, doesn't seem to have many close relationships, and used her teaching as an excuse not to live life. Still, she sounds stronger and more determined to win her battles than you – and I would never say it to her, but sometimes I wonder if she really is all that innocent – you, I have no doubts, you, Mark, were set up because of who you are, where you came from and where you are going. Do you think anyone at the top of the Board of Education wants a teacher smarter than someone running the show?"

There was a bit of silence.

Mark then reached for Ellyn to hug her, as a sign of thanks.

"What should I do?"

"You are waiting for a union to help you that doesn't seem to want to – maybe it's time for a new approach, someone who will talk with you now."

"I have been thinking the same," Mark admitted for the first time to anyone.

"Would you like to meet my attorney, Wayne Gray?"

Shortly after that discussion, Mark got the call he had been expecting and scheduled an appointment to see his NYSUT – appointed lawyer. Mark was excited, and Sarah went along with him, with the first glimmer of hope in months. Benjamin warned him to be careful, as did Ellyn, but nothing that anyone could say would penetrate. He knew that he would vindicated on all counts, that he was innocent. His case was not a case of classroom misconduct; Mark had found wrongdoings within a program outside the contracted school day. Mark had attempted a background check on this lawyer, but little was available online or through Benjamin's connections.

Mark met the attorney alone, as Sarah sat waiting for him in the reception area. The lawyer seemed cordial and interested enough at first. Unaware of the particulars in the case, he started his repertoire of questions and list of things that he would need from Mark. He told Mark that he would have to finish the meeting after an hour and that he would be in touch when he had more information.

Mark returned to Sarah, "This will be over with soon," she said as she gave him a kiss and grabbed his hand tightly for support.

"I hope so."

Mark called Benjamin to confirm plans that they had made earlier that day. They met at a downtown restaurant, quiet enough, yet busy enough to provide background sounds to avoid nearby patrons from hearing them. It was secluded enough so they could talk, review some papers, and take time to think.

"I told you so – I hate to say it, but anyone who has no vested interest, especially in a financial way, will never take the extra step," Benjamin said honestly, feeling bad, while not wanting to put Mark in a position of feeling worse than he already did.

Mark told Benjamin that that it seemed as his lawyer felt confident that he could do "something" for him, given his "relationship" with the DOE opposing lawyer. Benjamin had found out only that afternoon that in Education 3020a cases, lawyers from each side faced each other on case after case, in most cases with the same arbitrator, so there was much communication among the three. Some occurred behind closed doors and with no concrete evidence and witnesses to know if any deals were made behind any person who was accused.

Mark confessed that Benjamin was right. It was suggested that, since he had money, he should come up with resources to bring in expert witnesses, hire investigators, and help prepare his own discovery. He was told that he was the one who would have to produce and do all the work to make sure his witnesses would appear. If his witnesses did not show up versus the Department of Education, there would be repercussions on his results.

Benjamin told Mark his next step would be to carefully review all the discoveries the Department of Education shared with NYSUT and to make sure it was accurate.

Benjamin remarked to Mark, "You're lucky that students were not involved in his case."

"Why? Wouldn't they be good witnesses?"

"In most instances, yes, but in these cases, student records were not allowed to be presented, even if they gave merit to the accused. It was the same situation with parents, students, staff, and anyone who would testify against the Board of Education."

Principals would give these students a hard time and let other students, teachers, and lunch aides suffer academically and socially. It could range from simply ignoring a student being bullied by another student or falsely accusing them, punishing them with detentions, a student being yelled at in a class or ignoring phone calls from home. This was commonplace and complained about by defendants in each case. It was also something many involved in cases reported in their own blogs or shared with education reporters.

It also seemed as if OSI and SCI reports were not always accurate, since many interviews and documentations depended on multiple sources to complete an investigation. This issue was starting to become public knowledge as the media targeted principals and teachers who they felt should be fired before their day in "court."

"Mark, why don't you contact your appointed attorney and send confirmation in writing that you would no longer be needing his services and that you would be seeking representation elsewhere, Benjamin suggested. Mark had confided in him that Ellyn was ready to set up and appointment with Wayne Gray.

"Let's give it a little more time," and Mark refused.

When Mark returned home that night, Sarah was up, pretending to be reading the latest Sophie Kinsella novel, anxiously awaiting to some "quality" time with "her man". She also was ovulating , and thought tonight would be perfect for baby – making. Mark seemed tired and quiet, and not picking up her hints of joining her in a shower and a couple of hours of love making.

CHAPTER 33

Mark went back to his reassignment center in Queens and reported detail after detail to both Melissa and Ellyn at lunch.

Melissa was even more disillusioned. She kept interrupting Mark, discussing Juan.

"I know Juan will eventually take care of his child."

"Focus on your case," recommended Ellyn.

Yet Melissa went on, as both Mark and Ellyn knew she had yet heard a word on her case, and her stomach was getting bigger and bigger. One positive for her was that without lesson planning and grading papers, she had more time at night and on weekends to sleep and relax.

Ellyn once again offered to refer him to Wayne Gray.

Mark became defensive, and made the point that she was still there, even with a prestigious attorney.

"When does Wayne say you'll be out of here?"

By the conclusion of the conversation, despite all interventions to convince him otherwise, Mark still had confidence that the union would stand by him.

"After all, I am completely innocent." He believed in their strength.

Sarah could not concentrate at work that day. Behind Mark's back, she called Benjamin. Benjamin took the call and listened, but as Mark's friend, he could not betray their friendship, nor allow his professional conduct to be in question. He listened and then told Sarah politely that he would follow up and call her back.

Benjamin would not call Sarah back to give her the information that she wanted; however, he politely told her that he would keep supporting

Mark in whatever capacity he could, even if it simply meant listening. He had the perfect excuse: It was not his area of expertise, and he could not go against an appointed counsel that Mark approved of. Benjamin convinced Sarah of his points and told her that he would be there for her if she needed anything.

Behind their backs, and using complete discretion, Benjamin did a little of his own research and legal work. He definitely felt that something was not right. He knew from his own experiences that when someone was completely innocent, most of the time a settlement was reached before any public scrutiny. Why would the New York City Education Department, in connection with the state government, take such a risk of letting Mark, with his family connections and successful business, let this go on?

He never mentioned a word to Mark, but as he promised, he called Mark and made arrangements to meet later that week.

"I am going to bring a colleague of mine ... do you mind? She can use your advice."

Benjamin responded, "Sure, maybe she will actually listen to me."

Mark understood the sarcasm, but ignored it since Melissa had a twist in her case, and she did need help.

Somehow, several newspapers received an "anonymous" tip that led to a story about a "crazed teacher" begging for sex at the school and falsely accusing staff and making scenes for children and parents to see. It even included a picture manipulated to make Melissa look further along than she actually was. What made the story seem real was the fact that the assistant principal was quoted as saying Melissa was never a great teacher and was fighting with everyone, even within her own immediate family. Copies of the order of protection were clearly highlighted as well.

They met in Benjamin's office and then went to a local restaurant for dinner.

While Benjamin wanted to focus on Mark, he ended up listening to Melissa for most of the evening, and he took several notes; Benjamin was more determined than ever to help them out. Something smelled fishy, and it wasn't the school lunch. The discussion focused on Melissa's situation.

Mark and Benjamin tried to convey to Melissa that, since she decided to keep her baby, she would have to make her own health her number – one priority. She was only halfway through her pregnancy and had gained close to fifty pounds. Her OB–GYN was concerned with her weight gain and mental state; he told Melissa that she could develop diabetes or heart disease and that she was increasing her chance of miscarriage. She ate a full dinner and an extra – large piece of chocolate cheesecake all by herself, while the men had large chicken salads and simple sides with no dessert. They watched her in disbelief, even trying to discourage her from ordering so much, then trying to push her plate away, with no success.

Mark and Benjamin split the bill, shook hands and walked Melissa to her subway station. There, they spoke for a few minutes more.

"Did you call that lawyer you mentioned?"

"Not yet, but thinking about it ... Ellyn mentioned it again."

"Should I look for some others?" Benjamin suggested

But as usual, Benjamin was unsuccessful in his attempt to try to convince Mark to set up an appointment for a consult with one or two other attorneys. He would even be able to arrange these meetings for no fee, as a professional courtesy. Still, Mark refused. Mark confided he was actually going online looking into law courses and attending night classes. Benjamin told Mark that he thought it was not the right time, given his emotional state.

Melissa woke the next morning feeling quite sick. She called in to her supervisor, followed up with her school secretary, and then went back to bed. She had many days in her bank, but since her reassignment, had used up not only her allotted ten days per year, but also some of her days saved from previous years. She simply did not care. Nothing fit. She had no money for maternity clothes, and she hated the people surrounding her. They made it obvious that they were saying unflattering things about her and even some to her face.

By chance, Melissa's parents called her phone that day. She had ignored their attempts to reach her for days, but today was different. Melissa simply felt too sick to fight them, and the rings were giving her a headache.

Her mother was on the phone first, happy to hear her daughter's voice.

They exchanged a few words, and then Melissa's mother waved her dad to the phone and handed him the receiver. They would not take "no" for an answer and told her to expect them within the hour.

They got there and were shocked. Both of them wanted to cry, but held back the tears in order to support Melissa. They agreed to pack her up, take her to her doctor for a check – up, and then bring her to their home.

"You are coming home, and we are not leaving here without you," Her father demanded as her mother then continued, "We will take care of you and the baby."

They took her to her physician. The doctor told her she needed bed rest and sent a note via fax to the appropriate people. She stayed home the rest of the week. Both Ellyn and Mark called her, and so did her school personnel secretary. The secretary did not offer support: in fact, she told Melissa that even with her illness, the Board would not keep allowing her time off. She had to improve her attendance or face termination within the immediate future. She would be receiving a letter in the mail verifying the conversation.

Her parents offered her all sorts of help and even told her to give up her apartment and move home. They had a spare room that they were using as a library that they would renovate and make into a nursery. Given their past relationship, and also because Melissa was somewhat embarrassed by her current situation, she refused. They told her to think about it and that she could always change her mind.

Two of Melissa's cousins visited, as well as aunts and uncles. Melissa began to feel loved and supported, and now with friends like Mark and Ellyn, she thought that her future seemed brighter.

CHAPTER 34

A day came when Ellyn, Mark and Melissa shared a lunch with many of the other reassigned teachers awaiting disposition of charges. Brady, a first year teacher, started crying as he spoke: "My parents and grandma were teachers, and the only job I ever heard about growing up was teaching."

Nancy, a thirty year veteran, told a familiar story: "Seems many of the teachers who are over the age of 55 in my school building have been harassed over the past few years, so much so that many of them retired rather than go through the torture of dealing with incompetent bosses, no parent support and rude students that do not do their homework, bring their own supplies and show teachers respect."

"Why should they show respect? Government officials don't seem to. The union seems to allow it. And the media hates us," responded Christopher, another teacher.

"Not all teachers are having sex with their students the way the media makes it out to be," added another.

"And charter schools seem no better," Christopher continued. "They have advantages that we don't. They get more parent involvement and can reject a student's admission."

"We should all see that movie, *Superman*," the discussion continued.

"Or – how about *Won't Back Down*," chimed in other voices.

"I would love a mother to support me the way Maggie Gyllenhaal stands by her child."

"And the way she works together with a teacher."

Mr. White, the only teacher present actually accused of a sex act with students that were currently being investigated, put his two cents in: "Not all parents, students and schools are run that way."

"Yeah, you can say that – extra credit went a long way with you," responded Christopher. "How long are you here?"

The rest of the crew gave Christopher a look, for they knew he spoke way out of line.

White answered, "I am sitting in this 'rubber room' almost five years, getting paid, getting my pension, my health insurance, with no work to take home, no weekends grading papers or planning lessons, and you know what? They can run stories about me anywhere they want you can Google me all over the internet, and you know what – they can't prove anything. If anything, enough witnesses have already testified and backed up my story. So it is simply easier to let me stay here until I decide on my retirement."

Ellyn added, "He's right. He will stay here with a scarlet letter hanging over him because the DOE cannot bring criminal charges against him, and they can't let him return to a classroom for fear that if he does, someone will go after him, and he has enough against the DOE to win a major lawsuit."

Kit, a teacher who was actually going back to his school shortly, added a different insight. "You should read the actual complaint a parent filed against me about ignoring their son, the subsequent paperwork the union gathered about the student, and how they settled the case when my principal needed me back for test prep. That's it in a nutshell – if your principal needs you, chances are you will be back to teaching soon."

White answered, "You're in a unique situation – you got a quick response because you are also a parent in the community."

People in the reassignment centers who were there for investigations formed unique friendships. At first, each was skeptical of one another; they all wondered who would rat out whom, who knew someone who might be important, who was really guilty and who was really innocent.

Day after day after running into each other, having the same lunch times and feeling individual frustrations, they would draw attention to one another and form their own cliques.

Though seldom, occasionally someone left, and unless that person went right back to work, he or she typically was never heard from again.

It seemed like a revolving door. When one person left, one or two usually appeared soon, for accusations and investigations seemed rampant these days. Teachers and principals, now on the same "level" shared new friendships.

CHAPTER 35

On this particular day, Ellyn and Mark decided to vary their routine of eating alone joined a number of other teachers for lunch.

"Why not – it was such a nice day outside."

"Remember, just listen more and talk less," Ellyn reminded Mark.

It was a nice spring day, and the group decided to purchase their own lunches and meet in the nearby park, sit on blankets.

They were all sitting, nibbling their first bites and sharing chit – chats with those sitting next to them. As usual, the conversations stopped as the topic changed and everyone focused on one teacher.

One of the men was sharing some copies of e-mails that he had received from friends about some of the issues they found online and thought were helpful to him.

Parents, teachers and administrators joining forces and were discussing in detail how classroom daily instructors were forced to implement lessons with little insufficient training, class sizes beyond limits that offered quality learning, too much testing and unfair evaluations for students and others.

People within the system complained about excessive paperwork and the endless and needless documentation.

Buildings throughout the system, it was rumored, were filthy. Dust, mouse drippings, spills, pieces of broken glass, and rusty nails were visual sights in almost every education – related building. Bathrooms were filled with broken toilets seats, with broken soap, toilet paper, and towel dispensers. These items were never repaired.

"One teacher chimed in, "You should see how my desk is lopsided and I have to use books to even it out."

"My school happens to be clean, so I can't relate," added another teacher.

Then they went back to the paper.

Many complaints were that closets and file cabinets were filled with student records outdated over a decade and also with paperwork for curriculums no longer used.

It seemed that the worst part of all was that people within the system actually admitted that they had no idea what it was like to be a teacher in a classroom today, and lawsuits costing taxpayers millions of dollars were rampant.

The complaints in the papers that day were endless, and what was supposed to be a fun, relaxing lunch turned into a tiresome and depressing conversation.

They all realized that they were in the same boat. Each one went back to thinking about what he or she should do next.

"Let's eat alone next time," Mark suggested.

Ellyn agreed.

CHAPTER 36

Melissa was assigned a long – term project that she actually liked. She read background for a grant proposal for one of the Math curriculum coordinators, but the downside was that, since she was not allowed to use Board of Education computers, she had to hand write everything. Melissa wanted some of the information she found for her own future reference. She took home these notes and used her own copy machine and materials. She then used her home computer to send the information via e-mail to the appropriate staff.

One morning, Melissa showed up at work and received word that she was being assigned to a new desk on a different floor. Someone who had been sitting there for over seven years finally was able to retire with full pension and benefits and exoneration before a hearing. News like that gave Melissa and others hope. Her growing belly and realization that she was going to be a mother also gave her hope.

Meanwhile, Ellyn was still stapling, copying and coordinating paperwork and getting used to it. She devoted her time away from the "rubber room" to help Michael and the hospital raise funds for an innovative dental wing. She became PTA president of the community middle school where she lived. She re – styled her hair, went to the gym more often, and reshaped her body. Ellyn also began taking yoga classes, and the meditation helped her mental state.

Her relationship with Michael and the kids never seemed better.

Michael would be the contact for Wayne Gray for many reasons, the most important being that they all agreed that Ellyn and Wayne's office would have no contact while in any DOE building.

Michael signed the retainer and paid all the fees, so this would never be a conflict of interest, but Wayne had Michael and Ellyn sign a paper so that, if there were ever a fee dispute or change of attorneys, there would never be a problem with breach of confidentiality.

During a routine day, while Michael was in his office preparing for a trip that he was making the following week on gum diseases in connection with cancer in children, he received a call from Wayne directly. Typically, one of the younger associates would call, and Michael would return the phone call during his hour designated to returning messages, so hearing directly from Wayne was unusual.

"You and Ellyn must get to my office as soon as you can; we have to discuss something important."

Wayne wouldn't say more, and when Michael reached Ellyn, they thought the worst. Michael called Wayne back and made arrangements to meet the next morning.

That night, Ellyn and Michael thought perhaps that the Board of Education was willing to settle, since Wayne had told them initially that DOE would never fully vindicate. Ellyn had come to the realization that she was never going to teach again.

When they arrived in Wayne's office, they were seated in the reception area and overheard several voices speaking in a triumphant tone. They thought that it might be about her case, but without hearing the actual words, they could not be sure.

Wayne finally entered the reception area and gave Ellyn a big hug and shook Michael's hands with a big smile on his face. They entered his office to a conversation regarding her matter. Wayne Gray asked his secretary to put on the answering machine, lock the front door and join them.

In their minds, both Ellyn and Michael had thoughts of victory, but did not dare to even mention a word to each other. Then again, why wouldn't there be? After all, she was a victim.

They sat for a few minutes as the staff organized themselves for the next step.

Wayne leaned back as his chair reclined and picked up a handful of what seemed to be handwritten notes.

He finally spoke. "We are very lucky ..." He proceeded to discuss how, through their investigations and interviews with "people in the know," they were about to gather the information that they needed to destroy the credibility of superiors in the NYCDOE. They were able to obtain the paperwork needed to bring attention to the hiring of the principal, her background, and her ability to ignore both her own union, the teacher's union, and the DOE regulations and contracts simply through her connections made by family members. Not only that, but she had sexual relationship with many men, and possibly a couple of women, who would not want this information made public.

"The press would eat her alive ... they just featured her in the story about her cousin and used her pictures. A second scandal would have ripple effects," as associate added as he passed around copies of the recent article.

Wayne then handed over some of the documents to both Michael and Ellyn, and as they quickly reviewed them, their mouths dropped in disbelief, especially when looking at some of the pictures.

"The city will never allow this to go public." Wayne responded to their reactions with a tone of assurance.

Wayne then asked his associates to take turns explaining in detail some of the information they had obtained, with connections to the specific laws broken, questions of the chancellor's regulations being broken, and the direct connections to Ellyn. They even broke down details of how Ellyn's file was tampered with and how they could prove it. They had actual principal's notes versus official write – ups and pictures from school security with proof of daily classroom activity. Your former principal will back you up on all your successes.

"Here, take a look at what parents wrote about you. Also note how the at least two students backed up an incident you told me to investigate. If this goes public, parent would sue." Gray then shared copies of e-mails and Ellyn's evidence.

"If this goes to trial," another associate explained, "witness after witness would prove guilt on the part of the administration, district and TWEED staff." Apparently, there were a lot of complaints about the principal, not other staff, not students, just her.

One investigator had a tape of a staff meeting that he was able to obtain through a secret source that had Ms. Johnson threatening the entire staff if they did not comply with her rules, including grade changing, working beyond the boundaries of contracts, and even risking safety for all within school grounds. Most importantly, on this tape she tells how she was spending school money. Johnson was redecorating her office and eating in expensive restaurants. Receipts from these places, as well as sales – help and restaurant staff would prove she was misusing funds meant for supplies and equipment for student learning.

They then shut off the lights, set up a screen, and watched the video. Ellyn was clearly there, and, in fact, had spoken up in a face – to – face confrontation.

Wayne asked his receptionist to turn on the lights and told Michael and Ellyn that they, in fact, had much more. Because they spent the money on private investigators and shared nothing with NYSUT, they were able to accomplish their goal. Now, they had to sell it to the Board of Education to the level of scaring them enough to end this mess. If not, they would never settle and go to trial.

Since Michael and Ellyn had already suffered the negative results of intentionally distorted and hurtful media from the night of the fundraiser, making a 180 degree public example of how the school system really worked was something that they both were looking forward to.

By this time, Ellyn wanted to do this for people like Mark, and especially Melissa, and even the new acquaintances that she was now getting to know in Bayside. Even if they had guilt in their background, they were being treated like dirt now.

CHAPTER 37

Wayne looked through some papers, then put them down and looked directly at Ellyn and Michael.

"We need to have a press conference."

Ellyn quickly responded, "No, my children don't even know all that is going on ... and my parents."

Wayne broke in with "Ellyn, do you want to win? Or do you want to let the DOE know you are vulnerable?"

"I want to win, help Mark, Melissa and the others ... but there has to be another way."

Gray interrupted," Ellyn, the press got to you already ... the dinner."

They all looked at each other with dead silence in the room.

Gray was not getting the response he wanted, or needed.

Wayne turned towards Michael, "I'm wasting my time here. I have plenty of clients who need my advice and actually take it. We need the upper hand. We have it now, at least enough to show the public that a decent teacher, one who is beloved by her co – workers, students and their families and former administration is being falsely harassed and intimidated."

Michael turned to Ellyn, realizing that Wayne was right and that he had to convince her of that.

"Ellyn," Wayne continued, "I am representing a teacher who was taken out of the classroom for putting on her Facebook page pictures of a staff party with her holding a glass of wine. Is that fair?"

Michael gasped, "What, a glass of wine is healthy every night, isn't it?"

"And another who was taken out of his classroom because his wife got an order of protection against him. But what the media doesn't report is that the teacher and his wife are going through a nasty divorce and custody battle. Worse, she had an affair, and her boyfriend went to his house and hit him, trying to swindle more money from him than the court judge ordered."

"Disgusting" Ellyn answered.

"Then, do you want false information out on you first or even more embarrassment like they did at the charity event?" Wayne continued, "Or, do you want to play offensive and show the DOE you – and I mean you – mean business?"

Michael said, "Wayne is right – we have to rethink our strategy and play tough, or this nightmare will never end."

They agreed to think everything over and meet again the following Wednesday.

Exactly as schedule, they met, and rather than start with the usual updates on personal things, Wayne went straight to the issue at hand. "What are we doing?"

Ellyn and Michael looked at each other. The time had come, and they both nodded agreement. Wayne was to proceed as aggressively as he found necessary.

After the meeting, Wayne proceeded to call opposing counsel to discuss settlement. He left several messages that week, but received no return call. He suspected that they did not have a clue what he had and how far he would go, despite his previous record of success.

Whatever the reason was, he had to strategize. Meanwhile, Michael went about his business and Ellyn returned daily to Bayside without mentioning a word to anyone, including Melissa and Mark.

They met after work the following week to discuss further activity on the case. Wayne told them, without so much as a return call or e-mail, the ball was in their court. He was willing to go all the way – would they?

He suggested a press conference. He had done this several times before, so he knew how to set it up and who would come and write about it, even put it on the education segments of the local news nightly broadcasts.

Wayne told them that he would not give them everything; he would tease the public enough to tempt TWEED to settle.

Michael and Ellyn liked what they heard.

Wayne suggested that they send a clear message for why this happened to Ellyn to garner public sympathy and hinted at using the word "revenge."

Wayne also told Michael and Ellyn that because of their background, they were going to garner support from the general public. However, Wayne also mentioned that he could not control all of the media attention, and some would cause backlash about their lavish lifestyle, as it was so different from the majority of city public school families and many of those working within the education system.

They sat and talked and relayed several ideas. First of all, Wayne was going to play up all the fundraising and pro – bono work Michael and Ellyn did in connection to their dental hygiene procedures as well as other disabilities and diseases.

Wayne wanted to use their own three children's own scholastic and award – winning achievements, but Ellyn and Michael refused the idea immediately. No children, no office, no homes, and nothing related to their personal lives.

Each person in the meeting, including Ellyn and Michael, was assigned tasks to perform before the press conference was to take place.

The all knew the goal: Show the guilt of the system and the mayor. Present the real victims, the public, and Ellyn as the "puppet" of a broken, complex organization.

Ellyn's job was to get as many parents who would speak on her behalf at the event. Those she would ask would have proof of her work with them, and come from different years of classes and from different backgrounds. It was also important to show diversity in the levels and behaviors of students and how Ellyn treated each student and their family.

Michael's job was to gather Ellyn's awards, her bills from supplies that she had personally paid for, including the annual summer reunions, which few teachers, if any, ever organized and paid for, and her notes for volunteer work tutoring both in the after – school and hospital student programs.

Most importantly, until all planning was complete, nothing was to be leaked to anyone.

They set a tentative date to meet to finalize the execution of the exhibition, and the date and time of the actual conference, which was to be the following day.

Everyone worked efficiently and, by the final stage of planning, everything seemed to go without a hitch. Press releases were sent out following the meeting, and work was done in the reception area to welcome the guests the next day. Wayne's receptionist made arrangements to hand out press release packets with pictures and order the appropriate drinks and food so that Michael could pay the bill before the conference began.

Last minute touches were being completed. Chairs and tables were moved to fit a podium and microphones, and a screen for video to be shown. An hour before the conference, Wayne received a call from the assistant to the newly appointed President of the United Federation of Teachers. Somehow, the union heard about the conference and the leader wanted to know if he come and speak about injustices to teachers. Wayne politely declined and excused himself before more requests and questions could be answered. The president "smelled" something that could work for his benefit and had his assistant e-mail an offer of any suggestions or help he could "personally" give, with the unspoken assumption that he would get credit for his part and take recognition for the success of Wayne's work and Michael and Ellyn's money and sacrifices.

Wayne began the conference quite formally. "Ladies and gentlemen, we are here today because of two heroes, Michael and Ellyn Marks." He spoke eloquently about the trials and tribulations that brought them to this moment, and how the real victims were the taxpayers of New York and the children of the public school system, and not just in this city but across America.

Wayne used research that his paralegals had found in cases around the country and told the audience that copies of facts and surveys were available in folders by the receptionist's desk as they left. They had a personal farewell, and Wayne was able to make sure he had names, contact information, and individual send – offs to follow – up with.

Wayne was smart enough to emphasize the wrongdoings of Principal Johnson and not bring attention to Ellyn and Michael throughout his speech. He allowed video to compare the two offices, two sets of bills and receipts, and the time cards of Principal Johnson that the DOE used to pay her for overtimes and expenses.

Wayne also stressed the DOE's own documentation of the results of surveys from both the school community and the state – funded Quality Review, which both the state and federal government used as a guideline to support education.

He took a few questions, and with their permission, allowed two parents to speak and state their claims supporting Ellyn and admonishing the New York City Board of Education System.

Camera and questions flashed at Michael and Ellyn, and they responded with a simple "no comment at this time." When Wayne ended the conference, Michael, Ellyn, and their witnesses were quickly removed from the meeting room through a door into a small private office.

They stayed there until Wayne and his associates walked in almost a half hour later, after everyone had left and they could talk freely. Wayne thanked them and said that he thought it all went well. Now, they would have to wait and see until they heard from their opposition. Until then, Wayne advised everyone to talk with no one, call his office if they had a problem, and continue their daily routines. He assured them that this would be over soon, and that he had a very good feeling.

Ellyn took off the next few days. Both Mark and Melissa tried to contact her, as well as former co – workers and the PTA president. Michael cut his hours in the office to avoid calls there.

Four days later, while Ellyn and Michael were sitting at home together, Wayne called. He had received a tip from one of his press contacts that the Board of Education was trying to go after Ellyn in retaliation by destroying her reputation in the press. They were able to find nothing. In fact, they had found a contradictory reaction. Because Wayne had played up their charitable work, public sympathy sided overwhelmingly with Ellyn. They wanted their children to have teachers like her. Wayne gambled on the right formula for success, but he knew the quality of the people that he was working with and the money he had to "play" with for success.

Papers were drawn up, forwarded to Wayne, and a meeting was set for the following week. Ellyn's case was about to end. The Board of Education dropped all their charges, paid all of Wayne Gray's legal fees and expenses, and offered Ellyn a settlement for a million dollars, but with full pension benefits and insurances. They even offered her a job within the DOE at TWEED, giving her a title of teacher representative, since parents overwhelmingly sided with her, at least in the media coverage, and the system had to find a way to offer a solution to the criticism. In addition, Ms. Johnson was to be investigated immediately with the likelihood of a swift resolution which would probably lead to a termination and monetary damages to the Board of Education for misused funds.

Ellyn took the settlement, but refused the job. She could not work for the people and in the buildings that disrupted her life in such a way.

CHAPTER 38

"Never settle," Ellyn told Melissa.

"If Ellyn did it, we could too," Mark mentioned in a conversation, starting to think about making offensive moves, instead of just waiting.

However, she did not need to hear the words, Melissa was not settling. She saw how Ellyn had fought, and Melissa thought the case against her was weak because she was a highly effective teacher.

In most cases, before the media highlighted teachers in "Rubber Rooms," Melissa could have easily spent the next 20 years sitting in the reassignment area, and even though the rules changed and some teachers were fired, most would sit for years simply getting their pay.

Until this incident, Melissa had had a perfect record and a file full of documents and multiple sources who would call her a "great" teacher. She also was a union supporter, which was a big bonus.

However, with the order of protection, the newly added police reports, and the unexpected pregnancy, things had become complicated. She also took more time off than the ten allotted days this year, with about twenty in her bank. She still had over 50 days to "play" with, either using them while still on the Board of Education payroll, or receive funds as payment for those days upon retirement, also pensionable.

Melissa left her first meeting with her attorney feeling nothing. Her case was going to be before an arbitrator within the next few weeks, depending on the length of the two cases before her. If they settled, or went quickly, she could be in her hearings by the end of the following week.

A few days later, she received a call from her lawyer, telling her that one of the cases settled and that she should be prepared to go. More importantly, attorneys for both sides of her case had a conference call with the arbitrator. Based on the initial discussions, things were not looking good for Melissa. Melissa could not understand why, for this arbitrator had a history of being one of the few lawyers who actually supported union staff, and gave teachers lenient fines and punishments.

What Melissa did not know and was not able to find out, was that this arbitrator was having a "personal" crisis in his life. He was a married man having an affair with a much younger woman who had surprised him with an unwanted pregnancy. His girlfriend was pressuring him to divorce his current wife and then marry her. His wife and three college – aged children had no idea, and he had no intentions of destroying the "harmonious" life that he led as a leader in his community in a posh Westchester home, country and golf club and various other organizations. He also had no intention of paying alimony at this time of his life with no prenuptial agreement.

He had formed a personal bias against Melissa, or, for that matter, anyone who got pregnant, for what he felt was an intentional trapping of a man. Because no one who hired him knew of his predicament, he was able to participate in this case.

He knew that he was going to fire Melissa even before he heard the case, end of story. He was also going to use his influence to make sure that she could not work elsewhere. A little known fact was that although teachers who leave the New York City School system cannot work for them again, they can still be teachers in private schools or in public school systems in counties outside the city school system. They could also work in educational jobs like tutoring programs and educational supply companies. Many of these teachers, administrators, and former staff actually enjoyed and thrived in their new positions, and there was never an issue about being around children, following curriculum or cooperating with superiors.

In fact, certain hiring officials looked for people who had recently left the Board of Education since most had the materials and knowledge of the latest teaching trends and test – taking skills. That "Scarlet Letter" worked out to be an "A" for the many who were hired.

Life went on, but those in the "rubber room" would never think that way ... they were living in a past, fighting for a present and hoping for some sort of compromise ... because they could never forget this experience.

Ellyn called Melissa daily to support her and even met Melissa for a lunch at Melissa's mother's house one weekend. There, they had a conversation about Melissa's situation. Ellyn wanted to help her organize her defense.

Melissa sat with Ellyn next to a table with papers and files neatly arranged to review and discuss.

"Let's see what we can decipher here that and make four lists – one that includes DOE type of evidence against you – one that includes DOE evidence for you and two that are yours versus the DOE – and some of it will overlap."

Melissa handed Ellyn the order of protection. "I think we need experts on the various types of orders of protection. Wayne Gray mentioned clients that use them as ploys in divorce for financial gain – and although it doesn't relate here – we need to figure out why there is one in your case."

Melissa added in, "My cousin is a lawyer at Weil Traub, let's call her." "Hey Sandy, it's Melissa – tell me, what do you know about orders of protection?"

Sandy responded that "There are many types of orders – what exactly are you looking for?"

"Can I put you on speaker? My friend Ellyn is here. She has been wonderful helping me."

"Sure" and with that Sandy began telling her about orders of protection. "Orders of protection are no guarantee of safety – read the papers about deaths even after people file them. What doesn't make sense to me is that with all the things against you – nothing seems to be written about you with minors. Very odd."

Ellyn was sure that there was more to the story than she was hearing, but she couldn't offer realistic advice without knowing what wasn't yet being said.

A few days passed, and then Melissa received another call from her attorney. He wanted to meet again, and asked Melissa to bring her medical records, a list of potential witnesses, and a brief summary on each as to why they would help her case. They planned to meet the following week.

Again, before any details were discussed about the case, the lawyer stressed the fact that testimony would be based on phone conferences, and that the tone voice was important. The arbitrator wanted this case settled as soon as possible, because unless she had evidence to prove otherwise, he felt that her mental state could jeopardize any contact with children again.

The lawyer even suggested that Melissa could settle for a larger amount of money, getting her full pay and benefits for 18 months, and sitting within a reassignment center instead of actual roaming from school to school, which would alleviate more stress once the baby comes.

The lawyer used the fact that Melissa's story is the type of story media outlets would love to distort facts as a possible concern, even while making up facts and placing her picture on the front page with degrading headlines. "You should seriously consider the fact that you are going to be a mother; is this fair to bring your baby into this world, amongst scandal and pain?"

Melissa had a lot to think about.

CHAPTER 39

Melissa was getting more and more pressure to settle even before discussing the facts of her case. Her attorney sent her a letter and an e-mail detailing what he thought was the reality of her case; Melissa had an unwanted pregnancy and was alone, an image that the Department of Education did not want mixed into orders of protection from fellow employees. The letter stated nothing about her teaching abilities and her lack of a criminal record, and there was no mention of insubordination, incompetence, or misconduct.

Melissa read the letter with her parents, then to both Mark and Ellyn during different telephone conversations. They all agreed: Something didn't add up, but the choice was hers.

"Melissa, we will support you and the baby with any decisions you decide," her mother told her. Melissa was finally coming around and the thought of not knowing their grandchild was too much to bear for her parents.

She called her attorney and, without going into detail, informed him that she made a decision, and they had to meet. Figuring she was going to settle, the attorney made plans to meet late in the afternoon the next day. The attorney went to see both the opposing counsel and arbitrator beforehand and advised them that he was convinced he was going to have a settlement before the week ended.

Melissa came with several folders of papers hidden within a knapsack. The attorney, surprised, questioned her about the papers and accidentally mentioned they did not need any of that for settling.

"Why would you think that? Did I say that I was settling?" Melissa said angrily.

He looked at her straight in her eyes and reminded her that she was a young, smart person with a baby to consider. She could start a new career and family, and make a fresh start, perhaps in a new location where people did not know about the past or the situation about getting pregnant and losing her job.

It seemed as if he had no faith or interest in working on the case.

Melissa stood up and waved her hands out in disbelief. "Don't you get it?"

Melissa realized that she was in a no – win situation, but she refused to cave in.

"I don't understand – how can an arbitrator push to settle a case before we even have a hearing?"

"He seems to feel that you have no ground to stand on."

"That doesn't make sense," Melissa pointed out. "Has he seen my test scores, listened to a student or parent testify? What about my extra work, my awards of service and the fact that so many in the union know me and know how I volunteer for phone drives, participate in rallies in Albany and by City Hall?"

"Melissa, you were seen yelling at a principal and a staff person – two different unions to deal with."

"But they started with me – and they are lying."

"Do you have the money to really save yourself – then get yourself another lawyer. I get paid to do what I am told."

"I don't get it; you are supposed to be my lawyer – defending me, not my principal, who is lying through her teeth."

"I am just relaying what the arbitrator has suggested."

"Do all arbitrators give a verdict before a case is heard?"

"The arbitrators are backlogged; they try to settle all cases, so maybe I could get some more money, maybe another year's pay, let me see what I can do."

Melissa just looked, but did not respond.

"Listen, I have another client to see, let's talk in a few days."

Melissa did not say anything, but got up, shook his hand and left, thinking what a screwed – up system was in place.

When she left still determined to fight, Melissa's lawyer cupped his face, then went into the men's room and looked at himself in disbelief. What did he do wrong? How was he going to face the DOE attorney and arbitrator?

He tried to suppress his feelings and blow off the follow up after the appointment. He was able to do so until the following week. During meetings regarding another hearing, the arbitrator brought up the case with both sides of counsel amid discussion.

The arbitrator said, with conviction and in no uncertain terms, that he wanted the case settled. He did not say why, but when Melissa's lawyer wanted to discuss the matter further, he simply stated, "I made my statement; we have other cases to confer about."

Melissa's lawyer went back to the NYSUT offices and had his secretary draw up a formal letter "strongly suggesting" that she decide on a settlement package that would satisfy her needs, since it seemed likely that the case against her was strong enough for a termination conclusion. If she were to be terminated, all salaries and benefits were to end immediately, any funds owed would be gone, and she would have little to no chance of securing a job. Timing was also of the essence, given her personal circumstances, and there was a stronger need to get a job for the following term. Playing up the new baby situation was a great argument for his case because he knew that the situation would make it almost impossible to secure a position in any school or in any area of employment, since no business was likely to pick up her health expenses with the realistic prediction that she would need many days off.

That same week, Melissa got a registered letter in the mail from her landlord. There was going to be a larger apartment available in two months within the building complex. He liked Melissa and offered it to her at an "inside" price, which was actually little more per month than she was paying for her current apartment. It seemed like a great deal if she could secure the funds and made the decision before the beginning of the following month.

Melissa met with her parents. They still wanted her to move home and tried daily to convince her that it would be the best for many reasons: Help with the baby and lessening her living expenses topped the list. Melissa knew that they were right, but still wanted some privacy and wanted to maintain some self – respect through all of this.

She had a couple of weeks to make all these decisions.

CHAPTER 40

"We have a lot of decisions to make about what I should do next," Ellyn mentioned to Michael as he poured each a glass of wine after an exhausting day seeing patients, assisting their own kids with their homework assignments and conferencing with doctors who were taking care of Ellyn' dad.

Ellyn received multiple requests for media interviews, speaking engagements, and several business opportunities. Public opinion through media research wanted her to go back to teaching, and in the same school where she was chastised and harassed. For the first couple of weeks, Ellyn stayed low key. She went to each of her children's schools and activities and made complex homemade dinners every night. When Michael and Ellyn realized that they were being followed by similar cars for several hours, they called Wayne.

Wayne suggested that they go out of town, even out of the country, for several days, and that it would be better to take the kids along, until the commotion wore itself down. He told them that it would, and sooner than they thought, for stories in New York City change hourly, and another teacher could soon take over the front pages.

Luckily for Ellyn, Wayne was proven right, and on the very first day, they arrived in Turks and Caicos for five days of water sports, reading, family meals, and, most importantly, peace. The kids were old enough to stay together within the hotel compound and give Michael and Ellyn private time. Their oldest daughter even arranged a private dinner for them via room service, while the three teenagers ate at the five – star restaurant overlooking the poolside patio.

On the final day of the vacation, when Michael made his usual one – call – a – day to his personal secretary in the office, she relayed the message to contact Wayne as soon as he could, before he landed in Kennedy Airport.

When they came home, life seemed to return to normal, actually feeling a bit better. Ellyn had missed the routine of getting up early and having a place to go and a job to perform, but that was in her past. She had to think about what she wanted to do next.

One thing that she was determined to do was keep in touch with Mark, and especially Melissa. Ellyn told Melissa's mother and father that she would try to convince her to take steps in rebuilding their relationship and make life – changing decisions.

Ellyn invited Mark, Sarah and Melissa to join her and Michael for dinner on the following Saturday night, prepaying the dinner with Michael's credit card and arranging a car to transport Melissa to and from the restaurant.

Unknown to the group, Ellyn included Melissa's mother and father. Her goal was to have an enjoyable dinner and for the group to get to know one another without mentioning the investigation.

Mark and Melissa's friendship grew daily; given their current circumstances, it seemed logical. Ellyn was gone, although she tried to call them each weekly and be a positive mode of support. They still had New York University in common. They also did not completely trust the others still sitting, and especially not the newer reassigned staff, for lack of knowledge of their personal and professional abilities.

There was a rumor supported by newspaper articles (if they were accurate) that one of the newest to join the reassignment center inappropriately touched as many as two dozen third – grade boys and girls, with witness testimonies and a private lawsuit. Many of the accused teachers resented the fact that he was around, and all agreed that not only should he be fired, but in jail, considering what evidence and witnesses against him. He gave teachers a bad name. Their fear was justified when his girlfriend testified in court that he had fondled her young daughter, and scared the young ones; all the gruesome details appeared in multiple media stories with copies of the legal court transcripts.

Mark and Melissa made a mutual decision not to discuss the details of their cases. They became closer as they reminisced about New York University, fraternity and sorority parties, and life in lower Manhattan. They looked up old classmates, professors, and news stories about the time that they matriculated. It made each of them feel like they were twenty years old and innocent all over again. They spoke about how they would still become teachers, and how they would study in their education classes. They compared what they were taught versus what they actually needed to learn to become effective educators. To that issue, they had the same response: "Wow, what a difference."

They became closer as time went on without Ellyn, but they rarely discussed Sarah or their cases, and that comfort made them extremely compatible friends, nothing more.

Melissa's pregnancy was also a topic of discussion in a fraternal way in which Mark and Sarah could help her. Although Melissa and Sarah barely knew each other, Mark was confident that Sarah would be there for Melissa because Sarah was the kind of person who would help anyone in that kind of situation, especially someone that Mark thought so highly of.

That was how strong Mark and Sarah's marriage was, in spite of the thoughts of handling his situation putting a damper within their time together.

By this point, Melissa had developed diabetes and high blood pressure. She needed constant monitoring, a very strict diet, and plenty of bed rest. Her doctors recommended that she take a few days off, but her attorney told her that it would look bad for her case. If she wanted to look for future employment opportunities, her attendance records would reflect a troublesome future employee and deter her from any kind of quality job.

Mark suggested that she see a therapist, as he was, and called his doctor to arrange an initial meeting. Although she would best be served with simple sedatives and antidepressants, her OB – GYN discouraged them for the sake of the baby.

Coincidentally, as Mark and Melissa were building their friendship, for the first time Mark and Sarah were suffering in theirs. They rarely had sex, and when they did, it felt like an acrobatic act, with no kissing, hugging, touching, and soft caresses. They rarely spoke about important things outside of finances for their home and their own family needs.

As Mark was suggesting to Melissa to find professional help, Sarah was asking him to join her in a session with her psychologist. It came as a surprise to both that each had their own doctors and had sought professional help outside the marriage. What hurt more was that, in the initial conversation when Sarah asked Mark to join her in counseling, both realized they were keeping an important secret from each other. For the first time, something changed in their relationship. Both wondered what the other was keeping from them. How far were they willing to challenge their trust, their friendship? Both began to question their passion, realizing for the first time that their sex lives had changed as well.

They finally agreed to meet a therapist together and decided for the first visit to see Sarah's therapist, arranging an appointment the following week. In the meantime, they were cordial to one another, although, in reality, they were both walking on tiptoes around each other and being careful not to say the wrong thing or to instigate an argument.

When they arrived together, they were holding hands tightly and seemed as if they were leaning on one another, both physically and emotionally. The therapist started with simple questions, geared toward Mark, to answer about his family, childhood, and background, while taking notes and gathering thoughts for taking the next steps.

A half hour into the meeting, Mark confessed that he had been seeing someone since the 3020a situation began. The revelation of Mark seeking help seemed to give the doctor some hope for success with this couple.

CHAPTER 41

Mark and Sarah went for one more session together, and then both continued with their respective doctors on their own.

Mark seemed to discuss little other than his case in his sessions and started going less and less. He did not actually listen, nor did he complete any of the assignments that were asked of him.

On the other end of the spectrum, Sarah, who was never one to think that she needed help for herself in living with Mark's investigation, decided to go weekly; however, now that Mark knew, he graciously offered to pay for the meetings.

Sarah and her therapist reflected on the few meetings with all three of them involved. Based on the tone of the questions being asked, Sarah got the feeling that the psychologist began to develop a diagnosis on what was bothering Sarah and how to cure her.

Sarah was the victim. The victim that everyone forgets is the spouse, the parent, or the young child. Public investigations take a toll on them, too, and in every aspect of their lives.

Sarah was suffering from second degree interrogation. She knew people at work who talked about Mark behind her back; And friends that they used to go out with stopped making plans and severed contact by not responding to phone calls and e-mails. There were nights that Sarah did not want to go home. She never knew what was waiting for her. Would Mark be in a good mood? Was his mind occupied with serious thoughts about his case, or would he be working on his other business ventures? Would he be aggressive and proactive, or depressed and solemn?

Both sets of parents had dropped hints of becoming grandparents, maybe moving and investing in a home, and taking the next steps within their marriage, as seemed the natural progression.

Sarah lost sleep at night thinking about their future and about when this mess was to end. On several occasions, they participated in new activities and tried to have fun in art markets, fundraising marathons, and talks arranged by community groups. They were always nice and respectful with one another and seemed to have fun, but the one ingredient key to any marriage suddenly got lost. They were looking for that security blanket that their relationship in infancy so depended on.

One afternoon at the gym, a good looking man began talking with Sarah. His name was Guy. Without thinking, she continued the conversation innocently. He suggested that they talk some more and offered her some coffee at a nearby cafe, which she graciously accepted. Sarah thought nothing of it; after all, she had male friends from work, she kept in touch with male friends from college, and she even ran in the nearby park with one of her male neighbors. Probably Guy thought that she was single, as she never wore a wedding band to the gym.

During the conversation, Sarah found out that Guy was a doctor, a dermatologist, and recently divorced. His wife had left him for another man from work she fell in love with, and to add to the injury, she was pregnant with his baby. He stopped halfway through the conversation and apologized for ruining "the moment." He did not want her sympathy; he wanted her friendship.

"No need to apologize," she said. Guy continued talking about himself until he realized that he was dominating the conversation. He began to ask about Sarah. She felt uncomfortable opening up about her situation at home. Without realizing it, she forgot to mention that she was married, and Mark's name never came up. So, the tone of the conversation changed into reminiscing about childhood television shows and food fads. They talked for about 45 minutes, until Sarah realized that she had to meet Mark at home, so she thanked Guy for the coffee and told him next time, it would be on her.

She did not realize that Guy took her invitation to mean more.

Coincidentally, Mark was running late, so Sarah was able to shower and change, and by the time Mark's key made the familiar sound of his impending entrance, Sarah was ready, and looking forward to a quiet dinner with him.

Mark was in a pleasant mood; he had signed a deal that could make them a significant amount of money over the next five years, and he was excited to share the details with Sarah.

Mark brought Sarah a bouquet of roses and handed them to her as they greeted each other. "Hope you didn't prepare anything for dinner; we are going out."

This was the Mark that Sarah fell in love with, the romantic, soft – spoken, and business – minded person that wanted to share his success.

While waiting for their seats at the restaurant, Sarah excused herself for a stop into the ladies room, and Mark made his way to a stool by a crowded bar. He ordered a beer, knowing they had a wait ahead of them, and took advantage of the Knicks game on television. An attractive blonde saw the opportunity to flirt with Mark and made a beeline to the stool where he was sitting. She could have been Mark's type, a tall, natural beauty that most of the men by the bar would have been flirting if she would have accepted their advances. She started making chit – chat about the game, impressing Mark with how much she knew. The bartender handed Mark his beer. It seemed as if the woman was waiting for Mark to ask if she had wanted one, and when she realized that was not happening, ordered a glass of merlot for herself. She then noticed Mark's wedding band, but that did not stop her, for she knew men cheated, lied, and wore wedding bands for their own reasons if they were not even married.

Sarah finally walked out of the ladies room expecting to see Mark at one of the tables. To her surprise, she did not, and to her disbelief, she instead found Mark across the room involved in a conversation with another woman, an attractive woman with a glass of wine to boot. For the first time in her marriage, maybe even in her life, Sarah was jealous, but she could not let it show. Mark did not even introduce her to the girl, and as he waved Sarah over, he asked Sarah if she wanted a drink and kissed her on the lips. The stranger realized that she had made a fool of herself, and within minutes, Mark and Sarah were seated, discussing his new business venture. They went home and made love passionately for the first time in a very long while.

During Sarah's next session, she discussed the incident in detail.

CHAPTER 42

"Wow," Mark was saying as he helped Melissa pack boxes for her move to the new apartment, "you still have this from NYU – I threw mine out."

Mark picked up a pile of papers and started reading them.

"Melissa," he commented, "your students wrote the nicest things about you."

"What are you looking at?"

"Some letters – here's one from a mother: "Ms. Dobbs, no one, and I mean no one took the time and effort to work with my daughter. Even my pediatrician – who thought that giving her pills was the answer – couldn't get her to respond and develop her communication skills the way you did."

"I forgot about those," Melissa responded absently. She had her mind on the clutter that still needed to be packed.

"Maybe we should make copies and share them with the lawyers."

Later, Mark described to Sarah the distracted way that Melissa was behaving – as though she needed to get her move done, but really couldn't seem to focus on it very long without worrying about her case with the arbitrator.

"Mark," Sarah wondered, "why don't you let me help Melissa?"

"Because she is a mess, and she is really my friend."

"She is our friend – what's yours is mine, what's mine is yours."

"Does that mean I get that wacko at work, Victor – what's his name?"

"Very funny – maybe – he prefers men to women anyway."

"Seriously," Sarah continued, "there must be something I could do."

"She lives in a walk up, and her place is cramped."

"She is pregnant and going through hell ... she must think I'm some sort of narcissistic princess."

"Princess yes ... definitely not narcissistic, and most assured, all mine."

With that, Mark grabbed her and smacked one long, wet, passionate kiss on his wife.

Melissa had two weeks to finalize her move. She decided to enjoy her "luck" within the situation that her landlord had given her and take the new apartment. Despite their fears, Melissa's parents felt that they could support her decision, at least for the moment. They were starting to get along, and without telling anyone else, they were starting to daydream about being called "nana" and "papa." They also hoped that the baby would make them closer with Melissa, and as of now, with no father in the picture, they could have a major part in raising the baby. Also, they thought that even though Melissa was a single mother, so many children were living in one – parent homes that it would have little impact on her meeting a wonderful man who might eventually become a father to the child.

Melissa needed help in packing her belongings up. She accumulated so many materials connected with her teaching that she started to cry looking at the piles of papers and then the notes of others complimenting her work. She stopped.

Then she called Mark and asked him for his help.

Mark rang the buzzer around an hour later. They sat for about fifteen minutes and shared some casual talk. Melissa could have sat there longer, as she was tired and nauseous, but Mark came for a specific reason and had to leave by a certain time.

"Where should we start?" Both began in the two closets in the hallway, one with linens and toiletries, the other coats and storage.

Melissa thought that some of her older, no longer fitting garments could be packed carefully and given to some of her former students' families who were struggling in this economy.

Mark questioned her thinking. "After all of this?" Melissa responded that she had some contact with them all throughout all the difficulties.

"Why?" Mark asked, confused and a little angry with her. She did not respond and said that those belongings had to be packed separately, for she was definitely planning on giving them to some kind of organization, if not to her friends.

They bubble – wrapped a lamp and several glass bowls, and stacked towels and bed – dressing into boxes. Mark told Melissa to label everything carefully, as it would make setting up the new residence easier.

Mark lifted several worn – out and coincidentally outdated suitcases, since the materials they were made from were simply too heavy to travel with, and they were not on wheels. He started looking in Melissa's bedroom as to his next step. When he returned to the main sitting area, he saw Melissa on the couch, holding her stomach.

"What should I do?" Mark asked, and then realized he had no idea how to deal with pregnancy. He went to the refrigerator and took a bottle of water, suggesting she eat something as well. They took a short break, with Mark insisting that Melissa relax and just give him some direction as to what to pack and how she wanted it organized.

Mark saw how tired Melissa was and suggested they eat something. She resisted at first, but caved in. Mark opened her refrigerator and realized she had little in there to eat. He insisted on going down to the nearest deli to grab food and drinks. Fifteen minutes later, he returned with two sandwiches, green tea, water, and fruit.

Melissa did not realize until he left later that afternoon that she liked the companionship, even if it was just a friend. She could count on one hand how many times people were actually in this apartment visiting her, including family members.

Mark went home, and together with Sarah, drove to the North Shore of Long Island to have dinner with his parents. Few words were discussed about either of their days. They went home, made love, and watched an old Cary Grant film. Afterward, the television remained on as they fell asleep.

Mark went to help Melissa again the next day. Sarah offered to come, but Mark thanked her and declined the offer. Melissa was not her friend, just an acquaintance. He told her that Melissa was a mess, and it would likely be in both Melissa and Sarah's best interests to have as little to do with each other as possible. Sarah understood. Melissa could not relate to her, after all; she was married, working, and, even with Mark's problems, he was still making a nice living. Mark and Sarah had a family, friends, and a life outside of the New York City Department of Education.

Sarah suggested that Mark meet her at the gym around 5 that afternoon so that they could work out together and grab a quick bite out before coming home to prepare for the week. She would change around her plans and meet friends, visit the newest exhibit at the Museum of Modern Art, and buy his mother a birthday gift before they met up.

Mark took Sarah in his arms and asked her if she knew how much she adored her and how thankful he was for her in his life.

They prepared their belongings for the day, kissed goodbye, and went their respective ways.

Melissa was waiting for Mark with a door open and some lists compiled on the kitchen counter. Melissa went to give Mark a hug. Then they started to work. They had finished her bedroom and most of her living area when Mark suggested they take a brief break. "Did you eat breakfast?" he asked, thinking for sure that she had little in her home to satisfy herself, much less her baby and even offering him a snack.

Melissa surprised Mark by ordering beverages, desserts, and sandwiches from the nearby diner for the two when he arrived.

Mark was pleasantly surprised that Melissa thought about food and thought to himself that maybe she would take care of the baby, since many around her had formed unflattering opinions.

He moved toward the paper goods as Melissa tried to reach them and seemed to have "won the race" of collecting some plates, plastic silverware and cups.

As he caught the plates, they were standing next to each other and Melissa blurted out, without realizing it, "you know, you are the only one who really looks after me, and I can't thank you enough."

Mark did not read much into it, because he knew that it was not true.

CHAPTER 43

Ellyn looked at the calendar hanging on the inside of the kitchen cabinet connected to her desk. It was not as full as it always was – no post – its to grade papers, pick up a supply for a lesson or meeting with colleagues. It was her first realization that she really had little or no idea of what was happening in school. Ellyn reached for her cell and began to call the teacher she was closest to – as they both started the same year – and on the same grade.

"Nancy – Nancy, please call Ellyn."

Then she tried Glenn Warren, the gym teacher and as one of the few men on staff – the one who helped "his friends" when disciplining a "Child from Hell" who needed a strong male presence.

"Oh hi, Glenn! How are you?"

"Ellyn, it's good to hear your voice. Really miss you."

"So why haven't you picked up a phone? Anyway, what's doing?"

So trained, Glenn immediately went into shop talk. "School is hell, we are now all assigned hall duty during our preps three times a week, and when some of us called the union for some help, somehow the principal sent letters to files complaining of things like prep time requirements, hallway behaviors of staff and documents regarding respecting immediate supervisors, so that went nowhere."

Ellyn's response came with a chuckle, "Maybe you will be joining me soon."

Glenn didn't know how to respond, "Ellyn, I appreciate all you did to stand up for yourself, however I am not as strong as you. I need my job, my health insurance ... even my summer job, which there is a good chance I will lose because of the witch. I have to go. I'll call you next week. Bye."

Of course, Glenn never called, and neither did Nancy, nor anyone else. Ellyn even reached out to a parent she got along with, who was warned to stay away. "Ms. Marks, my child has been getting picked on by her teacher since you left. Please don't call me anymore."

That afternoon, Ellyn was standing in for her personal shopper to ring up her goods. "I really don't need much because my life is so simple now."

"Just try this on, it is new, but has a classic look, and it can be dressed up or with the right accessories, a casual day ensemble."

Ellyn ended up being persuaded for almost an hour to try on clothes, accessories and listen to her shopper bring her combinations that would make Ellyn look great.

"But do I really need all this?" Ellyn kept asking. "I wear simple skirts and tops to work and stay home more," thinking she might be saying too much, and then caught herself with "I'm older and just get more tired."

"Don't we all?"

"Let's go through everything and just take a few things ... and put away some." Ellyn didn't need to share that she felt guilt over not getting paychecks and paying Wayne expenses and some of his retainer.

"Then let me suggest this navy suit, and think about everything else. You'll see, you'll end up here next week. Why don't you give me your credit card, and I'll ring everything up while you sit and have a coffee?"

Ellyn reached into her handbag, pulled out her wallet, and grabbed her credit card, again, feeling the guilt of enjoying a pleasure while all this was going on.

Ellyn looked and felt better than she had in years. The finality of the investigation and the rewarding results paid off in the long run, except that she truly missed the classroom environment. She missed the days when she saw a child struggling with a math problem, or the happiness of success when another child reached a higher level in the reading program that was part of the New York City Department of Education's curriculum.

She missed her co – workers, who, one by one, were renewing their friendships with her. She even missed her summer reunions and the parents who struggled so hard at two and three jobs to enjoy the fruits of their new country and give a better life to their families.

She did not miss the rainy and snowy drives that would take her several hours each way, the days of informal observations that were biased and followed up with criticism after criticism. She did not miss the occasional student who became a behavior issue, nor the parents who taught their children to be rude, violent, and abusive.

She loved being able to take care of her home more often. She booked air flights to Florida to stay with her parents for several days and check in with her in – laws. She loved having more time to prepare meals, sit with the kids while they were doing assignments, attend more after school activities, and more importantly, spend time on herself and with Michael.

They discussed Ellyn going to work on marketing with Michael, even though he had since hired a capable firm and was gaining a national reputation. They discussed longer trips, trips to Asia, Middle East, and even an African safari. Ellyn was no longer tied to an unworkable schedule. They could travel at less expensive, less popular times of the year.

Still, Ellyn missed the daily routine. She missed the interaction with young children, something that her other work never brought her. She loved the challenges of meeting people that she would never have known; their customs, their religions, and hearing first – hand stories of growing up in lands so different from New York. She would often laugh at how the climates alone change a person and their outlook on a country's benefits.

Ellyn soon realized that she would not be happy going to daily lunches, socializing at the club, or living with a personal trainer at the gym. She already had those activities in her schedule and for her purposes, with enough time devoted to each. She watched how friendships changed by the constant togetherness twisted into malicious gossip.

Ellyn also missed her paycheck. They really did not need it; in fact, almost all of it was invested in several retirement funds and business ventures. Still, every couple of weeks, Ellyn had the ability to put aside money for her own use and feel a stronger sense of self – esteem; she had financial independence, something that many of her friends envied.

She was still young, healthy, beautiful and smarter than ever. What was she to do?

At least she would still be in touch with Mark and Melissa and offer them words of support.

CHAPTER 44

The week went by with no dramatic changes. Mark confirmed with Melissa that he would help her both days that weekend, as moving day was quickly approaching.

Sarah became angry on Friday night at dinner when Mark told her that he would be helping Melissa again. She had mentioned to her parents that they would visit, not knowing that Mark had made plans on his own.

"Just be happy that you are not Melissa – alone, pregnant, looking fat, dumpy, and with no real friends," Mark said as he tried to convince Sarah how lucky she was and how miserable Melissa's life was going at the moment.

"Tell you what, let's drive to your parents' place and take them out for dinner on Saturday, my treat," and he leaned over and kissed Sarah, thinking that she had already agreed.

Sarah knew that she lost this battle, but so had Mark; after all, she would win the war. Mark even convinced her that she should feel sorry for Melissa, and by night's end, she really started to feel bad for even mentioning to Mark her plans and apologized for her "childish behavior."

Mark left early on Saturday, leaving Sarah in bed asleep. He wanted to make sure that he had some time to rest and clean before the drive to Long Island.

When Mark arrived, Melissa was crying, and although she tried desperately to hide the tears, it was to no avail.

When Mark tried to get Melissa to open up, she simply would not. Mark knew that he did not have much time to waste, but she was in no mood to pack. In fact, she would just distract him. Mark insisted that they go to the corner diner to eat breakfast, sit, talk, and get back to focusing on the move. Mark felt bad, but she was simply not his responsibility. He did not need all this extra food. He wanted to help, but he also had his real estate business, his workout, his friends and family, and, most importantly, his wife to spend weekends with. Hopefully, today would complete his "good deed."

Melissa eventually calmed down, so much so that she was able to organize ninety percent of the packing and cleaning out with Mark's help by 3:00 p.m. that day, and she thought to herself that she was ahead of schedule.

Melissa did not want Mark to leave. Her telephone rang, and when she saw it was her parents, she let it go to voice-mail. They then tried her cell phone. They offered to stop by, suggested that she stay at their home, and even asked her to meet them for dinner – anything at all.

They called again about fifteen minutes later, and Mark insisted that she pick up the phone. "Don't put worries into their heads that simply aren't necessary," he told her. Melissa reluctantly took Mark's advice and picked up. She started responding "yes" or "no" to what seemed like several questions from her mom. Melissa looked over at Mark, who was bending into a big box, and he apparently did not notice the looks that she was directing at his rear end. Melissa whispered that she was going to excuse herself and went into the bathroom to finish the conversation in private. Within the few minutes of listening, Melissa got a few words in, like "I'm not alone," and "He's taping the boxes." This was misleading Melissa's father into thinking that Melissa was keeping news from them and maybe the father of the baby was actually getting involved, or maybe that Melissa was seeing someone. Either way, her father finally gave in and said his goodbyes as Melissa kept mentioning that she was too busy for this conversation and had to finish up.

She returned to the living room area, where Mark had started assembling a new box and clearing the rest of the belongings in that area. The place looked empty, with the curtains coming down next. They decided to tape newspaper over the area that brought sunlight directly into eye contact, and then the room would be done. They continued to work. Mark looked at his watch, as he wanted to get home in time to clean up before going out. He even daydreamed about some romantic time with Sarah.

CHAPTER 45

"Wayne, you have a phone call from someone with an accent that I can barely understand; what should I do?" the receptionist buzzed in complete confusion.

Wayne received calls like this often, especially after a high – profile case ended with loads of positive press.

"Take a message and tell them I will call them back, and get all their info."

Wayne was surprised by his receptionist, as this happened all the time.

But she buzzed again. "Wayne, he's being persistent about speaking with you and refusing give me details or give me a phone number for you to call back."

"Ok, tell him to hold a few minutes and I will take the call, but Linda, no more calls like this."

Wayne made him wait a few more minutes as to see if he was serious. He finally pressed his speaker button.

"Wayne Gray here – how can I help you?"

"We need your help."

"Before I can help you, you must be able to calm down and tell me your name. Are you in a jail or police station?"

The gentleman calmed down. Wayne heard him take a deep breath and take a moment of silence.

"Forgive me, I am just so upset. My name is Dr. James Julius Edwards. I am a parent at the school you just won the case against. I have met with several of the parents of the school where Mrs. Ellyn Marks worked, and they want to sue too. Do I have your attention?"

Wayne told him yes and continued the conversation; this gentleman would have to realize that suits cost money and take time. Wayne was feeling him out to see if he was serious, asking him if he could afford a case and if he realized the consequences of pursuing it, all without giving the doctor details.

After a few minutes of discussion, Wayne realized that he had nothing to lose by meeting him briefly late in the afternoon or early evening for an initial consultation.

"I have to prepare for a court appearance later today, so I am going to ask you to think about what I told you."

"There is nothing to think about, when can we meet?"

"I'll connect you back to my secretary and she will set up a free consultation. I really have to go now, but thank you for thinking of me."

Two days later, at about 5:45 in the evening, the buzzer to enter the reception area rang. The receptionist allowed Dr. Edwards in, along with fifteen other adults.

"Wow, he is serious," was the first reaction of the receptionist, and as she was preparing to leave, she contacted building security that they should be on alert for a small group of people meeting with Wayne, and based on some past experiences, they should make themselves visual with unannounced visits to the office periodically.

She asked the visitors to sit and wait for Wayne, and then she headed directly into Wayne's office.

"Wayne, I think this guy is serious, very serious indeed, because you didn't mention to me he was bringing a small army to this meeting."

"What are you talking about?"

"Check for yourself. There are over a dozen people here, all signed in as parents from Ellyn's school."

"What? Are they nuts? I never said I was taking a new case."

"I called security to come up and keep an eye out, and I also put the Rinaldi file on Peter's desk for review for tomorrow. Don't forget you have to prepare for the Weinstein settlement meeting for Friday."

"What would I do without you?" Wayne smiled. "Okay, tell the army I will be out in a few and have a good night. By the way, tell your husband to take you to a nice steakhouse on me and have a happy anniversary."

"You remembered!"

"Of course, I did. Next to my own, it's the one I have to celebrate most, right?"

"Good night, and good luck. They look like a hungry bunch and ready for the kill."

Wayne went into his private bathroom adjoining his office, washed up, gargled mouthwash, and prepared for a good first impression.

Five minutes later, refreshed and ready to start the meeting, Wayne opened his office door and made his way to the visiting area entrance.

"Dr. Edwards, what a surprise. You didn't tell me you were bringing the school," joked a smiling Wayne Gray as he reached for the elbow of the doctor to give him a strong, powerful handshake.

"You didn't think I was kidding, did you? I told you we had to meet."

Wayne led the group into a large conference room. There were beverages and individually packed snacks by the corner counter and an ice and water machine. Wayne never questioned these purchases years ago because they were invaluable for unexpected meetings as this one seemed to be.

They were a few chairs short, so several of the gentlemen followed Wayne to the other conference room and brought chairs back. They took about fifteen minutes to organize, settle, snack, and make informal introductions.

Wayne knew that he had to have complete control of this meeting or it would go on all night. He introduced himself formally and handed each visitor a package with background on the firm, staff backgrounds, and recent cases written up by various media outlets.

Wayne explained, before he heard anything from anyone about class action cases, that this case would be difficult to prove, harder to win, and cost more money and time. This was true even if they mutually agreed to work together on this particular case on a contingency basis. In fact, any law firm would ask for money upfront, perhaps a fee with five figures and expenses paid in full as bills piled up, such as court reporters, court filing fees, unexpected research, and witness fees – the list could go on.

Wayne advised the crowd that there was first a test, and to his surprise, the room was dead silent. No one reacted to what they just heard.

So, Wayne did the next best thing. He introduced Dr. Edwards to the group formally and as his initial contact on this case and simply stated that he had five minutes to share with the entire group why he wanted to sue, who he wanted to sue, and to convince Wayne that he was their man.

Dr. Edwards took out some notes and first thanked Wayne for his time. He stated the facts as he and the others saw them. The City of New York, the Mayor's office, the Department of Education, the United Federation of Teachers, even as high as the White House, if any Federal funds were used and laws were broken, should be sued for the violation of any and all quality of education rights, and it was the right of parents to protect their children.

Overall, the group was orderly and polite. They went around the table and introduced themselves. They were a diverse group from all backgrounds, different occupations, family situations, and financial abilities.

That was a plus for Wayne, as was the fact that he already had so much background on the players involved and the school history. This would save him time and money.

But then again, that is why they called Wayne in the first place.

Several mentioned Ellyn and her case, but most stated their stories, their children, and their anger with the educational system.

Wayne was tempted, but would not let his interest show. He told them that they needed $25,000 to start, and upon picking their representative, that person was to contact him and let him know which way they were heading.

CHAPTER 46

Melissa took the day off that Monday, as she was tired and nervous about moving. She had thought all weekend about how the move was making her "more motherly," and questioning her choice about keeping the baby. While it was too late for an abortion and there were no choices in adoption, her parents told Melissa that they would raise the baby and legally take over guardianship for her. Once she felt comfortable enough, they would return rights to her.

She spent most of the morning in bed, daydreaming about motherhood and, surprisingly, about companionship with a man. She closed her eyes and thought of herself in a passionate embrace with a handsome man; he had a muscular body and would whisper kind words in a gentle tone. She saw no face, just the mere existence of the man; it was a man that she felt close to, yet he was so far away. Around 11 AM, she texted Mark, asking him what he was doing and if he could speak for a minute. As usual, Mark was working on his private paperwork for his business. He would go home and transfer to the appropriate files on the computer and make the phone connections he needed to fulfill his obligations successfully there.

At this point, Mark was making a nice six – figure salary while sitting in the "rubber room"; his parents, uncles, and aunts, and even Sarah had mentioned to him to that he should resign and move on. However, Mark's pride and determination to find out what exactly happened and who was actually stealing from the Department of Education got the better of him. Mark dreamed of the day that he would celebrate and say to the world "I told you so."

"Mark," Melissa's voice on the phone was strained. "I know I have taken so much advantage of you, but you are the only one I trust and you are the only one who doesn't question my every move. Can I ask you one more favor?" Mark knew what was coming.

Mark actually did feel sorry for her, not just because of the pregnancy and investigation, but because she had such low self – esteem and lived in a world filled with scenarios that she created that would never come into fruition.

He agreed to come over after working at the reassignment center, but for only a couple of hours. Mark made it clear that for the rest of the week, he had other commitments that he simply could not miss or change.

Melissa showered, dressed, and even put on makeup.

Mark arrived a little after four o'clock. He put down his knapsack, took off his jacket, and said, "Let's roll."

Melissa's packing was more complete than she thought. Mark could not understand why she thought that she needed more help, but, knowing she was so unhappy, he agreed. He had mentioned to Ellyn during their last phone conversation how much he was helping her. Ellyn responded that she was surprised that nobody else was there, since Ellyn knew Melissa was reconnecting with several family members, and Melissa never called her directly.

Melissa sat on the couch to take inventory of what was now four corners with many boxes, a few larger pieces of furniture that the movers would cover with their blankets and tie up, and just a few belongings that Melissa would pack as she said goodbye to this part of her life.

Still on the couch, Melissa let out a painful "ouch." Mark immediately went to sit by her and asked what was wrong. She told him that she felt a crack by her left shoulder and on her side. Without thinking, Mark went to rub the area where Melissa said that it was hurting, just as he would have for Sarah. With his hands, he targeted the spot where he felt the tension and tried to ease her pain. Boy, does this feel good, thought Melissa. It was so strong, so intense, and so careful, as if by a professional; yet, this was better, because he was a friend with real hands and real muscles, so unlike those in her dreams.

They sat for a few minutes with Melissa's back toward Mark when, all of a sudden Melissa turned around and leaned into his arms, then even more. When their chests touched, she leaned in and, without a moment to spare, kissed Mark. At first, Melissa kissed him on the cheek, but then deep into his mouth. With both of their eyes closed, Mark imagined

Sarah and for a few seconds responded and even moved more into it. He enjoyed what he felt for the brief encounter until he opened his eyes and realized the truth. It was not Sarah, it was Melissa, and he immediately pulled away. She held on to him, eyes closed and mumbling something that he did not understand.

"What are you doing?" Mark asked, and Melissa responded in a surprised tone, "Haven't you done this enough before to answer that yourself?"

Mark was in shock. What had just happened – and why? "I have to go, I have to leave now, I'll call you later," and without so much as a look back, he grabbed his belongings and left, shutting the door loudly. Melissa tried to call after him, but he ignored her. Melissa told herself that he did not hear her and he had shut out everything around him.

Mark tried to reach Sarah, but the call went directly to voice mail. He felt numb and cold … what just happened? Why did he kiss her? How long did he respond? Did he start it? No, he would not, but did he? Was he giving Melissa any hints of interest? Why was he helping her in the first place … and why only him, why not her cousins, her neighbors, even someone her parents could hire?

Mark was distraught with guilt. He kept asking himself questions he tried to answer, and some ideas seemed off base. What had made Melissa kiss him? He started thinking that Melissa was definitely misinterpreting his kindness, and he was angry, angry with Melissa, but angrier with himself.

What about Sarah? Did he love her enough? Was there really a problem in their relationship? He still desired her more than anyone else. Did she still feel the same about him? Did she ever think about or act out a kiss with someone? Would she? Could she?

Those thoughts and images he had imagined during what seemed like an endless subway ride made him especially angry.

Mark arrived at his stop, walked up the long set of steps, and realized that he was not ready to see Sarah.

He stopped by a local bar and watched television while pouring his sorrows into a beer and watching the New York Yankees lose a game; they had been winning until the bottom of the eighth inning.

He tried to escape his thoughts of what happened and about Sarah, but could not. His beautiful Sarah could have any man that she desired. He knew it. He knew that several ex – boyfriends followed her on Facebook, and he could see how men looked at her when they were out. He mentioned several times to Sarah how guys were "checking her out" on the various machines at the gym, but Sarah blushed and denied it.

What an epiphany.

CHAPTER 47

Mark's anger became his answer to a question that he never thought that he had to answer. Maybe he had never had to answer it because he alone knew, and he never had to question it before. He had felt it on his first date, during their courtship, as he walked down the aisle on his wedding, and every moment since.

He loved Sarah deeply. She was his best friend, his most exciting and most important lover, his reason for existing and succeeding. He had not kissed Melissa because he had been thinking about Sarah, but that did not matter. He realized that this mess was making him less of the man that she deserved or wanted.

Should he simply resign and let everything go? His life would be much less complicated; Mark could be his own boss and make his own money, much more in fact, on his own terms. He could also be involved with more people on his level, both intellectually and financially. Mark could travel as he pleased and hire and fire as it was necessary, and he would treat those around his work much more professionally than any union or school administration.

Mark thought to himself that maybe Sarah thought that something was going on with Melissa. They had this horrible situation in common, and he was spending both quality and quantity time with her when he could and should have been doing activities with Sarah.

Mark still was in the bar and realized he had to go home soon. He walked his way to the men's room and washed his face. He glared into the cracked mirror and knew his next move. His eyes were red, and he noticed a few grey hairs, something that had never bothered him before.

He returned to his stool, where the bartender had saved his drink and place, and left a twenty – dollar bill on the bar top. Mark then proceeded to the door. Next door to the bar was a Korean deli with a flower stand, and he immediately took out his wallet to purchase two dozen roses.

Expecting Sarah to be at home, Mark took a deep breath as he entered his own apartment building and greeted the concierge with a big smile and wave. The concierge responded with a remark about the roses and told Mark that he had a package for him, but he would hold it until Mark had a free hand to carry it up.

He put the key in its hole and thought he heard Sarah inside walking over to the door, but was surprised to find that Sarah was not there. He walked around the apartment thinking that maybe she was in the bath-room or on the phone in the bedroom. It was a shock for him to see that Sarah was not home. Now, his imagination was going all over the place; maybe she was out with someone who spent time with her, someone who was kissing her. Maybe he had lost her. This was not good.

He proceeded back to the dining table and laid the roses down. He then sat on the couch and put his face in his hands. How could he ruin the best thing in his life?

The phone rang, but Mark ignored it. He simply could not move. He even felt a tear or two fall.

A few minutes later, Sarah walked in.

Sarah saw Mark, said hello, and walked straight into the bedroom with several bags from the boutique that she frequented on Second Avenue.

She said nothing else, and she did not see the roses.

He composed himself and gave her time to settle in. Mark then stood up, put the roses in his hand, and proceeded toward the bedroom.

Sarah was changing out of her work clothes into a t – shirt and was bending into a dresser drawer for a pair of sweatpants.

Mark grabbed her from behind and pulled her close to him, surround-ing her stomach with the roses.

"God, you are so beautiful," Mark whispered, as he began nibbling her ear.

Sarah took it all in, and she was surprised and found an unexpected bout of happiness. She turned into his chest and felt at home. They kissed passionately, deeply, and slowly. Sarah missed the passion and thought-fulness that she fell in love with. Neither could believe their sudden luck.

No words were necessary. Both knew exactly what was going to happen next. The roses fell to floor, separating into individual stems with some of the petals separating. The dampness of the stems stained the carpet, but neither noticed.

Mark and Sarah made their way toward and onto the bed, which seemed warm with a heat that had been lost for months. They touched each other slowly, reintroducing themselves to each body part; the softness of Sarah's skin, the roughness of Mark's chest hair, and the flow of blood in each giving new colors to the veins and capillaries. It brought back the days when they were first dating, and while they took their time to enjoy each and every embrace, time stood still.

They kissed, wanting only to please one another, which at some points seemed impossible since each was reaching new heights of pleasure. Suddenly, Mark pulled Sarah underneath him with strength and separated her legs to go way deep inside of her; they both experienced multiple orgasms together for what seemed like an eternity.

Their love was real, inside and out.

Sarah finally made the first move to end the embrace, as she needed to use the bathroom and wanted to clean her face. She was sure that her mascara had run when she felt tears of joy.

"Don't leave," Mark begged.

Sarah told him not to move and that she would return within minutes. Before she went back to bed, she went to the kitchen, filled a vase with some water, and tried to salvage what was left of the beautiful roses that Mark brought.

She had never used their Baccarat vase, a wedding gift that they were both afraid to use and break, but now, nothing seemed as important, even if the crystal fell and broke into millions of pieces, for their hearts were sewn into one piece of love.

She crawled back into bed, still completely naked. By then, Mark realized that they had not eaten dinner, and it was late, but this was Manhattan. "Should we grab some dinner?" Mark questioned.

Then followed up with, "Wanna go out?"

Sarah made a face that gave Mark the impression that she wanted to stay in. All that "exercise," though, made both realize that they were famished.

"I could scramble some eggs," Sarah suggested.

"I don't want you to fuss. It's getting late – I'll just order up some Chinese." Mark proceeded to order their usual as Sarah stayed peacefully under the blanket.

He found a bottle of Moet and Chandon and two wine flutes in a den area cabinet and put them in the freezer for a quick chill.

As their order arrived, he put on some sweats and opened the door.

He gave the delivery boy the money, grabbed the champagne and flutes, and took it all into the bedroom.

They fed and toasted each other and sat on the floor awhile, eating slowly and actually leaving most of the food untouched. Mark leaned over to wipe a hanging piece of rice from Sarah's hair, and when he leaned over her body, he spilled both glasses of the bubbly and began kissing her again. That led to another round of lovemaking on the floor. They actually began to fall asleep there on the floor, but Sarah shook Mark enough to tell him to get into bed. They slept like bunnies that night and spooned as they never did before.

The next morning, the alarm clock rang as usual. Neither wanted to leave their bed, but neither could miss work.

They fulfilled their morning routines, and before Mark left, he went to kiss Sarah passionately, told her that last night was great, and thanked her. He also told her that when they got home, they needed to talk.

Sarah could not figure out what was on his mind. She was hoping Ellyn's ending rubbed off on Mark. Maybe Mark was finally going to hire Wayne Gray, and take this case to a new level or simply resign and end this mess.

CHAPTER 48

After Mark left Melissa's apartment, she sat and cried for a long time. She finished all she could and stayed focused on her pending move.

She thought nothing of the kiss, nothing of Mark, but needed to pack and get out of there.

When she finally sat down, though, her mind drifted back to the kiss with Mark.

Mark had been kind to her, and helpful. He was always there to pick up a phone or come out of his way to pack. He never brought his wife; in fact, it seemed like he never mentioned her. Sometimes, Mark did not wear a wedding band, and he certainly spent time with Melissa on the weekends, picked up his phone at night, and always had a smile on his face whenever they were together.

Mark had made it seem as if he were giving her vibes that said he was interested, and in time, Melissa thought perhaps that he would come to her and admit them. But for now, she had to say goodbye, and if nothing else, after that kiss, it was perfect timing.

Melissa sat on what was left of a couch, unwrapped and ate one tub of chocolate chip ice cream and two large bags of barbecue potato chips.

She drowned her sorrows in her appetite, but the baby reacted negatively to her feast, and Melissa was up most of the night in the bathroom, using what was left of the tissues to clean her mess.

No one called, e-mailed, texted, or made any kind of contact with her.

Melissa was alone.

CHAPTER 49

Luckily for Mark, Melissa was taking off the following day to complete her move. He did not call her, and she guessed that he was not going to follow up and help her. Melissa, despite being on a tight budget, realized she had no other option. She hired workers to move her into the new living quarters.

Melissa had to stay focused that day, and Mark was nowhere in her mind, her words, or her actions, except when she once glared at the deli where they had picked up food. She wondered what he was thinking to himself now.

Mark was not thinking of Melissa in the slightest, but he knew that he had to tell Sarah what happened.

Meanwhile, as she was moving, Melissa got a call from her NYSUT attorney. Melissa was told that there was a good chance her case was coming up soon and was asked if she would consider accepting a settlement before the hearing began.

That night, Mark made several decisions. He sent a text to Melissa. "Hope your move went smoothly… are you coming in tomorrow?" He did not let on that he knew that she had completed her move, nor did he dare to ask her a question leading her to misinterpretation.

Melissa was not thinking about anything but her new home and the settlement offer. She thanked him for his help and told him that she was tired, that she just wanted to do her job and to go home.

What she did not want was a lecture from Mark about the kiss, and how it was all her fault, because he did put his tongue down her throat and stayed there quite a while.

Mark changed his tone of voice when he saw that he was not getting anywhere. Soon, he would need to speak to her in person.

He apologized for not coming over and going to the new apartment. He made up some story about a family emergency and apologized again for not finishing the job as he promised. By getting her off track, he was able to get Melissa to agree to meet him for lunch at a Chinese take – out several blocks away, which was quiet and secluded. He told her to meet him there, he did not want anyone seeing them walking together at this point. He made up a story about how he had to complete a filing project. In reality, he had made about fifty copies for one of the Human Resource directors that he liked very much, which took about fifteen minutes, and read a James Patterson novel. In actually, he merely skimmed it, and really had no idea what the plot was. Mark was playing out the lunch appointment in his mind, and what he had to say.

Mark arrived ten minutes after Melissa. She waved him over to a table as she bit into an egg roll. She also had a can of soda. She finished chewing and called to him to order, as she already had. Watching her chew on the egg roll with the knowledge of what he had to say took Mark's appetite. He ordered a soup and a seltzer. While he was paying, Melissa's food was ready, and he brought her an oversized plate filled with what looked like a spicy steak, fried rice, and another drink. Normally, he would have paid for her, but after the kiss, he held back. He carried the tray to her, then went back for his food.

"Thanks for meeting me, you look good, considering all that's going on with your move," Mark stated. He wanted to sound friendly, but firm.

Knowing that they had a limited amount of time to talk, and that he wanted everything said and understood during at this meeting, Mark sipped some soup, bit into a wonton, then put down the container and began to talk.

"I'm sorry about the other day, but I love my wife very much. Sarah is my past, present, and future."

He would not let Melissa interrupt which she tried several times. He made it clear that what happened was a mistake, a big mistake, and that it never should have happened and never would again.

He even made it clear that he had never thought about or touched another woman since he met Sarah. Melissa felt that what he said was not true and talked herself into thinking Mark was lying.

She was going to say something, but did not. She had him there now and was afraid he would get up and leave.

She ate and ate and finished everything in front of her.

Mark watched partly in disbelief, partly because she had eaten so much and more importantly because she had let him speak; whether or not she actually listened would show up in future words and actions.

Melissa said nothing except when she looked at her watch, realizing that she had to leave a few minutes earlier than he did. Melissa cleaned her tray and said a friendly goodbye.

Mark was done; he ate half the soup and took the beverage with him.

Since Melissa was pleasant at lunch, he agreed to walk with her back to the DOE building, even go in the elevator with her, with security and others there to witness them together.

A security guard overheard him, "Melissa, we are always co – workers and partners in this ... remember that." And they entered the elevator.

Both got off on their respective floors, said nothing, and went their separate ways.

Melissa was given a task to complete before the time she signed out. Luckily, it was counting papers and sitting down. She brought a pillow for her legs and a step stool to put her feet up.

She had no time to think about the lunch with Mark.

That night, alone in her new apartment, Melissa's imagination starting creating vivid glimpses of life with the baby and a man. Then she swung her brain into the lunch with Mark.

She thought of herself in sexy lingerie and poured herself a glass of red wine. One glass of wine would not hurt the baby.

She sipped slowly as she refilled the glass with another liquid, her tears. Melissa was so unhappy, and so alone.

She accidentally spilled a sip of wine on her breast, and tried to get the stain out, along with rubbing some potato chip crumbs off her chest. She got up, walked into her new bedroom, and looked into the mirror, which still needed to be hung.

Then, she felt the baby kick. She rubbed her stomach, which seemed like one of her few motherly instincts. She rubbed, and then cupped the bottom of her extending belly, as if she were holding the baby. She began to sing a lullaby in a soft tone.

She rubbed her stomach in a curricular motion. Then, Melissa began to talk to the baby, as if it were already there, and in a serious tone.

"Kid, it's just you and me. First your dad, then Mark, and even all those people who once were so happy for us, they are nowhere to be seen. We are here, all alone."

Melissa grabbed a tissue and blew her nose.

She went into the bedroom that she was preparing for the baby and looked around at the bubble wrap, boxes, and empty walls. Even the color gray left by the previous renter screeched "alone."

Melissa made a decision, a very important decision.

The next morning, Melissa followed her usual routine, punching her electric time card in the machine at work, reading a novel while putting her legs up and thinking in between chapters.

At about 11, she reached for her cell phone and proceeded to call the general phone number of the NYSUT offices.

She left a message for her attorney to return her call: She was ready to settle.

Very quickly, and the first time for such a prompt response, Melissa received a call back. Her attorney sounded as if he truly cared; his tone and words were different from almost every conversation that they had had in the past, either on the phone or in person.

They made an appointment to meet. This was the one time that the attorney was overly busy with his cases and a recently departed lawyer's cases as well; for better or worse, the earliest that they could meet was later in the following week.

However, as soon as the phone contact ended, the attorney immediately called the arbitrator and suggested that they plan a settlement meeting.

The arbitrator told Melissa's attorney to make the appropriate arrangements with opposing counsel and send formal notification to all necessary parties.

Whew, did I luck out this time, the arbitrator was thinking. He indeed felt lucky this time, but who knows what could happen when a teacher does something that could hurt his professional and personal life in the future? Could this arbitrator save himself then?

The papers were drawn up and e-mailed to Melissa for review, and most of the cookie – cutter settlement requirements were highlighted: no work within the NYCDOE, no future lawsuits in civil court, no public media attention, and various confidentiality requirements.

Although unhappy with the situation, Melissa felt she had no choice for her and the baby.

CHAPTER 50

Mark thought that he would tell Sarah what happened almost immediately; however, every time he tried to get into a serious mood and talk, Sarah looked and smelled so good that they went into sex mode everywhere, even in a restaurant unisex bathroom.

He brought up Melissa's name a couple of times, and each time, Sarah would stop him mid – sentence, suggesting how he should help her, and what a good friend he was. Sarah even offered to help. "Why don't you tell her to call me, or give her my cell phone number?" "How about I arrange a small baby shower for her, tell her to e-mail me some names and e-mails…"

Mark at first resisted, then starting thinking that maybe Sarah could help him with Melissa, as a team.

They went together to Sarah's therapist and discussed the "Melissa situation" – everything but the kiss.

He could not. He would not. Should he?

The therapist found a newfound togetherness in both of them and gave them several assignments to complete before they met again.

They planned family dinners, kept separate diaries with thoughts of their conversations, activities, and physical contact.

They each planned "date nights" and even discussed a European tour for three weeks that upcoming summer.

One thing that Mark did not share was a meeting with Melissa that he planned after work one day, for coffee. Melissa was cordial and very matter – of – fact when accepting. She had the settlement on her mind and had decided not to share her intentions with anyone, including Mark.

"Hey stranger, how are you?" Mark asked in a happy voice as if they were buddies who hung out daily.

Melissa did not respond quickly. In fact, she did not respond at all that day.

Mark suspected Melissa was still upset with him, but wanted to make sure that they met. As he signed out for the day, Mark texted Sarah that he needed to hang with Melissa for a while and should be home by 5:30 that afternoon.

"Just remember, no hugs and kisses," Melissa joked a text back with a smiling face, not realizing what she just wrote.

"Not even Hershey's," he wrote back, then proceeded downstairs.

They met by the corner and walked a few minutes away to a small mall with several fast food establishments. They settled on a small café, and Mark made Melissa take a seat while he put in their orders and paid.

He got all the food and paper goods and even wiped down the dirty table. That comforting and protective side of Mark made Melissa break down immediately.

"I'm settling my case," she blurted out.

Mark was shocked. "Why?"

Melissa went on to say that they made an offer that seemed like it was too good to be true. She was unhappy, but had to think of the baby before her own needs.

They spoke calmly, and Mark told her that both he and Sarah would be there for her and the baby, that she was not alone. Melissa wanted that more than anything and promised that what went on with the kiss would never leave her lips, ever. It was not that important in the grand scheme of things.

Melissa thanked Mark and suggested that all four of them, pointing to her belly and laughing, get together soon. Both felt great relief and hope for a strong friendship in the future.

"Maybe I can't fight anymore," Melissa continued. "I actually think I was set up, but who would believe me? Everyone thinks that I had consensual sex with multiple men and that I am a slut. This baby deserves more."

Mark went to give her a hug. "Sarah and I are with you all the way."

Just then, Melissa received a phone call from her NYSUT attorney. "I better take this, thanks."

To her surprise, she received some interesting news.

Her settlement was on hold. The DOE attorney had to take emergency leave and return to his family home in Georgia to care for a dying mother. Melissa's case had to go into a reassignment pool, which would take a couple of weeks, at least, to get the new attorney on board and updated on all the information.

"Just sit back, and hold tight," the attorney passing on the message continued. "This will end soon enough."

Melissa was upset, as she had finally made her decision and now had to wait. So was the arbitrator, who desperately wanted this to end, but could not show any reaction to this unforeseen change. He could not bring attention to himself.

CHAPTER 51

Mark and Sarah entered the subway station, used their Metro cards, and ran into a closing door heading in the downtown and outside Manhattan area. They reached the new apartment building, called up for Melissa to buzz them in, and realized that she lived on the first floor, which was good for a new baby.

Sarah and Melissa had met briefly several times before, but never without a group, nor had they ever engaged in meaningful conversation. But, as soon as the door opened, Sarah embraced Melissa with a warm, tight hug. It was almost like sisters reuniting with a comfort and trust shared by few. Mark waited a few minutes until he joked and mentioned something about joining this "threesome." He joined the hug, then all proceeded to tour the new place.

The space was bigger, and there was a private room for the baby. Melissa was quite lucky that this apartment had come up, and on top of that, the owners of the building liked her and arranged for her to have the space for the same amount of money that she was paying at their other rental building.

The superintendent had told the owners over and over again that Melissa was quiet, helpful, and rarely had guests, much less random sleepovers. To them, none of this made sense.

They sat for a few minutes by the dining area and spoke about everything going on, especially about all the things Melissa needed to prepare for the baby. They did not discuss either's case.

Then Mark broke up the talk. "We came to help, so what can we do?"

Sarah looked around; there were so many boxes. The answer was obvious. "Let's start unpacking." She asked Melissa if she had cleaning supplies, and Melissa showed her what she had brought from the old apartment. It looked like they would need more cleanser, towels, cloths and a new duster.

"I'll run to the supermarket we passed getting here and be right back."

"Let me get some money."

"That won't be necessary – consider it a housewarming gift," Sarah responded.

And, on that note, Sarah left, and Melissa and Mark started to talk. They were both grateful for each other's trust and apologized again for what happened. Melissa mentioned that her family was coming over that weekend and invited both Sarah and Mark to the housewarming party. She would be ordering pizzas and using paper plates, and her cousin would be coming over earlier that day to help set up and buy drinks, snacks, and dessert.

"Nothing formal, I really can't at this stage."

Mark answered immediately that both he and Sarah would love to come.

Sarah returned as Mark was moving labeled boxes into their assigned rooms. Melissa was always organized, and she was always known to be well – prepared and admired for it.

Through all of this, that characteristic had never changed: her reassignment notes, her daily logs in Queens, all her baby information, doctor's records – she was still on top of her game with organizing details and paperwork.

They started with the simple stuff, like the bathroom, with the toiletries and shower curtain. Mark hung it up, and they realized that Melissa needed new bathroom goods like a garbage can, towel ring, and a small rug.

Sarah and Melissa were washing out the refrigerator and kitchen cabinets together when Melissa's phone rang. She answered quickly, thinking it might be one of her family who needed to finalize details for their upcoming visit – and then stood frozen, stunned, paralyzed by the stumbling, almost incoherent voice on the phone. Sarah noticed immediately Melissa's look and waved for Mark to come immediately.

In a few moments, Melissa gathered her wits enough to put her phone on speaker and hold it out toward Sarah and Mark, her face a combination of fear and amazement.

" – ha muerto, mi madre, mi madre, ella ha muerto," the voice was saying, repeatedly. Melissa finally gathered herself enough to say to Mark and Sarah, "It's Juan – the baby's father. He keeps saying his mother is dead."

Mark's long experience in dealing with changing business situations kicked in suddenly, and he mouthed to Melissa, "Ask why he's calling, what does he want?"

Sarah looked at Mark confused, "I thought that they had no contact."

"Juan," Melissa interrupted the broken voice on the phone, "I hear you, and I'm sorry for your loss, but why are you calling me? Juan, you haven't spoken to me in months!"

"I know, I know," came back Juan's voice. "But mi madre, she told me so many times I must make it right, this thing that I kept struggling over, she said again and again I must be as my father and she would want me to be, and – oh, I do not know, what must I do? What must I do?"

Melissa stared at Mark and Sarah, still too stunned to make a response. Mark took the opportunity and whispered again. "Ask if he will talk with me. Tell him I am your friend and will advise him."

Melissa spoke briefly into the phone, and gradually the broken, tortured voice on the phone slowed and waited. She held the phone out to Mark.

Melissa went to sit down; her heart was beating quickly, she held her head as if a bomb had just blown up, and she had to hold on for dear life. Her world was about to change, but in a different way than previously expected.

When Mark had made the necessary arrangements with Juan, they stopped unpacking; cleaning the apartment had become the last thing on their minds.

Melissa wanted to call her NYSUT attorney, but knowing that this development was too important, Mark insisted that they had to play this safely in order get Melissa fully vindicated in the right way.

Mark thought that he should speak with Benjamin first.

Melissa called her parents and asked them to come over to discuss this discovery.

Within an hour, all parties were meeting in Melissa's cramped apartment. No one cared that it was not set up, too small or stuffy it seemed.

Benjamin told them to have Ellyn contact Wayne Gray on his cell, he would answer immediately for her or Michael. Mark then put Juan on the phone and Benjamin gave him strict instructions

"Juan, now there are witnesses and evidence, an attorney will be hired shortly – you are going to have to meet with the appropriate law enforcement officials – you are not to have any contact with anyone connected to the board of education. Is that clear?"

Michael texted Wayne, who agreed to meet with Melissa first thing the next day. Melissa wanted everyone there to be with her as she was about to show the world that she was not crazy, violent, or a slut. She was a professional, an example for the youth that she met and mentored … and she was about to have a baby because of an illegal act.

They also agreed that Melissa should not be alone that night, nor discuss anything with anyone. She went back to the island with her parents. Her parents were so grateful for the help from their daughter's friends that they wanted to treat everyone to dinner, but other commitments kept Michael and Ellyn from going. Sarah and Mark also declined. They felt that Melissa needed time to be with her family. This latest development changed everything, including their relationship in the future.

No one was able to sleep that night. Melissa kept crying tears of joy, and as she spoke to her belly, promising that she would never hurt her child again.

CHAPTER 52

Melissa's parents brought her to Wayne's office, where they also met Ellyn and Michael. Mark and Sarah both went to their respective jobs and did not want to bring any attention to what was going on downtown in the law firm's reception area. The surprise visitors to the office that morning, but not in the meeting, were Juan and the attorney from another firm Wayne had enlisted to provide separate and independent representation for Juan, whom they expected to be arrested as soon as he made the agreed statement to the district attorney's office later that morning.

Wayne got a head's up from both Ellyn and Michael about the circumstances in both Melissa's professional and personal life. He was hungry for the case for many reasons. Wayne already knew the outcome: he would garner more public attention in a positive way for both more clients and as a "boutique" firm, and finally, he simply hated the Board of Education and their teams of union attorneys. Wayne hated how they had manipulated innocent people, engaged in their legal practice with a lackadaisical attitude, and how they did what they were told, regardless of the fact that people were innocent until proven otherwise.

He desperately wanted this case; together with Ellyn and the luck of their New York University connection, this case was media platinum.

Wayne invited everyone into his office. They all sat down, spoke to one another, and made the appropriate introductions. Wayne suggested that, in order to make this case stick, he would need an investigator and specialist to verify the events and keep track of any evidence gathered by the inevitable police investigation, to do background checks, and to force DNA testing. He would not charge them money, since after confirmation and taking this to a favorable settlement, he would garner all the media attention needed. Wayne would also want Melissa to cooperate with him fully and stand by him during the press conferences and in all media interviews.

But most, Wayne pointed out, they needed the verification that Juan would provide in a written statement.

All of the initial expenses incurred within the next couple of days, Melissa, and if necessary, her parents, would have to pay up front and directly to their service providers. But as Wayne reassured them, the money would be returned as part of the settlement.

No questions were asked, and the retainer agreement was signed by Melissa. Then, a contact list was made, and calls were made with everyone listening in. As it turned out, by the end of the work day, Wayne received calls back with all the pertinent information that he needed.

It also turned out that the assistant principal was a friend of Alex Donovan, the young gentleman that Melissa befriended at the executive board of education offices early in her career. He was the one who got Melissa the job at this school after she had been manipulated by the administration of her first job and forced out. He knew that if he needed anything from Melissa, she would oblige, and if a problem would arise, Terry McNulty would back him.

Alex Donovan could no longer hide the truth, once Wayne Gray was on the case.

For someone like Melissa, this was a life – changing event, with harmful ratifications on both ends. What was worse, the government had endless funds, media contacts, and multiple employees, so no matter how many of these cases came to a settlement, the winner was always the government. Knowledge of wrongdoings by government workers and hiding their injustices was something that the government was usually able to manipulate.

Gray was building a consistent repertoire of clients with situations like Melissa's, and he knew how to build his reputation on having his David – and – Goliath – type win many times over.

With Melissa, he now had something else: rape, pregnancy from the violation of her body by two government employees, and a cover up, supported by the poor investigations and conclusions by the Department of Education.

Wayne had to explain to Melissa that she needed to follow his lead and to purposely use her pregnancy to garner media attention and public support, for it would only better her negotiations for settlement, both monetarily and emotionally.

Wayne also had to be careful not to make himself out to be an "ambulance chaser" in the eyes of the public, building cases where information might not be 100 percent accurate, or just handling these types of cases for money and publicity.

But this one, it was iron – clad, and with Juan's and Alex Donovan's statement, he had it firmly in his pocket. Would Melissa fully cooperate?

CHAPTER 53

Meanwhile, uptown, a business – sized envelope was being delivered to Mark and was placed in his locked box while he was reading a book in Queens.

Sarah got home before Mark and put his pile of mail aside. They never opened each other's mail, text messages, or e-mails. They had complete respect and trust for one another. Mark came home tired. He tried calling Melissa to find out what went on in Wayne's office, but her phone went directly into voice-mail. He then called Ellyn, who told him it was best not to speak on the phone, but things were looking good for Melissa and would end in her favor shortly.

Sarah and Mark went to the gym together, grabbed dinner while they were out, and began to prepare for the next day. As Mark was getting ready for bed, he remembered to check his mail. He opened the sealed envelope to discover a letter from an attorney's office with an attached contract relating to one of his newest ventures for distributing some goods for the family business. He put the papers down, slid into bed, and cuddled Sarah until they both fell asleep comfortably, and within a very short time.

The next morning, as Mark was grabbing apples from the refrigerator, he realized that he needed to contact his father to ask how he should proceed. He put the letter in his backpack, kissed Sarah goodbye, and went to the subway station. He bought coffee and oatmeal from the deli across the street from the DOE building. They knew him well and sometimes gave him extras because he was always so friendly. Mark also bought copies of both the New York Post and Daily News for sports updates (he and Sarah had the Times and Wall Street Journal already delivered to their apartment).

After he clocked in, he tried to contact Melissa, but she texted back that she would not be in and was very busy and would try to call Mark later on. Her supervisor came over to Mark around 10 a.m. that morning to question him about Melissa's health and her baby. Luckily, no one suspected anything but her health. Then, the supervisor brought up something that seemed somewhat unprofessional. "You're friends with her, you know her case is ending, what's going to happen?" Mark felt extremely uncomfortable and tried to hide it. "She's just sick … I've haven't seen her in a while." With that, Mark changed the topic and said something about the Knicks. He knew that his supervisor was a fan, and they spoke for a few minutes about possible trades for next season, and then Mark excused himself to go to the bathroom.

When Mark returned, he removed the letter from his backpack and reread it. He did not like to bring personal business here, but he was not doing much work, and this task was timely. Before he sat down, Mark realized that his water bottle was empty, and decided to fill it before getting involved in his work. Mark kneeled down and put the letter away, not putting it back in its envelope, and by accident, left the zipper open.

After Mark walked away, the supervisor, wanting to ask him another question about Melissa, walked back to Mark's cubicle. He saw the open bag and the paper with a firm's logo on it. He looked around, making sure that Mark was nowhere in sight and that others were not looking at him. Then he picked up the letter and started to read it. He put it back and left before Mark or anyone else could realize what he was doing. He made a U – turn for the stairway, did not want anyone to see him wait for an elevator, and ran straight to his superior, the head of the Queens system and one of only five deputies with direct access to the mayor.

The supervisor shared with his boss what he saw and asked his boss what he should do.

His boss thanked him and told him not to say or do anything. Things would surely be taken care of.

When Mark returned to his cubicle and bent down to get the letter, he thought it odd that the letter was turned over the wrong way. In a rush, he thought, maybe he had left the zipper partly open with the letter exposed. He decided to put it in his pocket and review it over lunch to make the appropriate contacts. He noticed a small stain, and realized someone indeed went into his personal belongings and read this.

"Benjamin, I can't be sure, but I think someone here went into my backpack ... and read a letter they shouldn't have."

"Mark, it's time, call Wayne Gray." They planned to meet.

"Don't do anything," Wayne told Mark when he called, "just call in sick and get to my office. I will rearrange my schedule to see you at 11 today."

Mark called his parents and Sarah, updated them on everything and called in sick.

Benjamin met Mark at Wayne's office for emotional support.

"I told Mark not to go with the union attorneys or trust anyone." And, just as Benjamin said those words, Mark's attorney called and Wayne suggested that Mark pick up so that he and Benjamin could listen in.

"We should meet, given the newest events involving your reassignment." Mark only listened and told the attorney that they could not do anything until the following week. He needed time to think and compose his emotions.

The attorney understood and knowing Mark's case was going nowhere, soon agreed.

Wayne Gray complimented Mark on his composure and professionalism, because deep down, he knew that Mark was scared and angry.

Mark reviewed the previous day's events, remembered and retold in exact detail what had happened, and his curiosity surrounding his opened backpack and letter reversed.

Wayne was decisive about their first response: "We are going to have to subpoena the school for all their security tapes to confirm violations to your privacy laws in your past and current locations. They will love that."

They worked out a plan. Meanwhile, Mark was to go in the next day and try his hardest to act as if nothing was wrong. By the end of the week, Gray would have everything set in motion.

Sarah and Mark met with her parents in what was a prearranged dinner, since they had tickets for the latest Broadway musical success "Once."

Mark explained that, according to Wayne, a new set of federal and state laws were now broken under invasion of privacy acts and harassment laws, and this would all end soon, and in Mark's favor.

Mark spoke with assurance, putting up a decent front, although, on the inside, as Wayne Gray's had said, he was angry and scared.

CHAPTER 54

Wayne had two timely and unexpected cases to serve, and it was by sheer coincidence that they had several common themes, most notably their New York University connection, their innocence, and being set up for failure.

On top of that, Wayne had a court appearance, planned months ahead, and several notices and paperwork on deadline that week. He also received calls to meet potential new clients. Most of the work had to be handled and overseen by him, even with his associates working closely. The work made for twenty – hour days, and Wayne had to rearrange everything.

Wayne knew that he had to commit time to both Melissa and Mark and try to tie them together. He was able to get an adjournment on his court appearance; nothing was happening on that case, anyway.

As for meetings with new clients, he had his associate call them, tell them that he could initially meet them, and take it from there. In a way, that was good, since it would weed out real cases versus vendettas and see who had money, who would work with a team, and who understood that, if their own case was on deadline, Wayne would be there for them. All too often, people refused to believe that they were terminated for reasons that were justified, and maybe that they were not working up to a standard considered reasonable and within a guideline of competency.

CHAPTER 55

Unknown to Mark, attorneys and the arbitrator had been reviewing his case informally. Many felt it was a "cut and dry" case.

Apparently, people in "higher" places knew and respected Mark, and thought it wise to review all the documentation in his case before going forward with it formally. They took their time. Besides, many knew of Mark's family and their ties to influential leaders in many areas. Let Mark make this salary and just wait.

Arbitration hearings were not what the public would expect. They ran very "long" hours – if starting around 10 a.m. and usually ending by 4:00 in the afternoon, if that, with several brief breaks and a lunch hour could be considered "long hours." There were exceptions to rules, depending on the ruling of the hearing officer and availability of both sides' attendees, especially that of the defendant.

Arbitrators were paid by the day, some as much as several thousand dollars, and pay was based on their resume and travel time. Additionally, they were paid for research and reviewing and the final write – up of the case, and since no one was actually overseeing them on a regular basis.

While the speculations or charges claimed that Mark deliberately tampered with documentation involving funds, there was no actual proof of funds in his name, bank accounts, or even his signature on anything remotely related to the disputed paperwork.

With the latest press on his personal finances, and his ability to profit during "rubber room" time, would this change the case?

A conference call was held without Mark's knowledge. Apparently, Mark's father and uncles had made contributions to several charitable organizations and political campaigns throughout the years in the name of the business and in connection to both professional and social friends that had ties to the mayor. The mayor, somewhat unpopular these days for his inability to control taxes, unemployment, and the rise in crime, did not need any more negative publicity or more allies turning into opponents. His staff member in charge of cases like these within the Chancellor's office was informally contacted and discreetly told to "handle" the situation accordingly.

And so, while Mark was awaiting word from Wayne, playing dumb with his union attorney, and trying to keep up appearances with Sarah, his family, and especially those around him in Queens, a private conference call was about to take place.

The call took no longer than 15 minutes. The word was clear: Take advantage of the recent media, promote the fact that Mark should not be making money while sitting in a reassignment area and getting full pay and benefits while he was still not exonerated from his investigation. It would be important to make the point that most teachers were not in his predicament, and almost all teachers never go through the trials and tribulations of reassignment, fines, and termination. However, in the end, Mark was not to be fired, nor face a harsh punishment. And then, they had to make sure that he stayed within the system and somehow garnered some publicity with the mayor.

Mark received a call from his union attorney; he was about to start hearing procedures the first of the month, which fell on the following Tuesday, less than a week away. Mark listened, said little, and proceeded to jot down some notes; he was frustrated and surprised, for there was no mention of meeting for any last – minute discussions or sharing any more information. It was briefly mentioned that the hearing would be starting around 10 in the morning, and they should meet briefly beforehand, arranging to meet in the NYC Department of Education location on Banks Street around 9 a.m.

Mark was polite, thanked his attorney for his help and agreed to meet, giving no clue what he was thinking or what he thought was about to happen.

Mark then left his cubicle, walked down the stairs to exit the building, and called Wayne, updating him on his latest information. Wayne did not seem surprised.

"Mr. Gray, it's Mark Ollins. Would you believe that I finally heard from the union. My case is about to start hearing procedures."

"Of course, they figured out you smelled a spy in your bag. Tell you what, go ... see what they say ... but remember, take notes and keep quiet. I will take over after that."

CHAPTER 56

Wayne Gray suggested to Mark that he go to his hearing and say nothing, as he would be the last witness to be called, and Wayne would have his case finished before anything could happen. The first day of any hearing involved opening remarks by both attorneys and some strategy to see if the case would settle and from all sides, which an arbitrator would be leaning in his rendering a final decision.

Wayne could not stress enough for Mark to keep quiet, stay as calm as possible, and take notes, mentally and physically.

With most other clients, Wayne would have never gambled, but Mark was a professional businessman and knew how to read minds and work opposition. Wayne clearly made no bones about it: Mark was not to mention anything to Sarah, his parents, or to anyone else for fear that they would cave under pressure if suddenly questioned.

Wayne was right. The first meeting took a little over three hours, with a small bathroom break, and a closed – door conference among attorneys and an arbitrator. The opposing counsel on this case was a newly hired lawyer, recently appointed to Mark's case.

Since Wayne had explained what the day would bring, Mark knew exactly what to expect. The DOE attorney based his case on one topic, the documentation for an after – school program that Mark worked for, and how he had knowingly and with intent planned on benefitting financially from the program. To their surprise, the DOE did not bring up the recent incident in the reassignment center or the follow – up media coverage.

The union attorney had a decent opening with several facts about Mark's teaching abilities and professionalism that simply could not be ignored. Mark's work had been published in education magazines, including the union's publication, and parents had awarded Mark, on several occasions with gifts that were given to him in ceremonies that had been taped and documented.

There was nothing that the DOE could do to avoid Mark's past.

In addition, parents, students, and co – workers had volunteered to testify, write testimonials, and do whatever they could to help reinstate Mark quickly and vindicate him. This hearing could run like a circus if the presiding officer lost control of it.

The arbitrator asked for lists of potential witnesses, Mark's personnel file, and copies of all discovery demands made by both sides. It took a lot of paperwork, a lot of research, and a lot of billing time. Because of scheduling conflicts and the background information that the arbitrator now needed to review, the case was next scheduled for the following month, but to stay within the new guidelines of finishing cases, the case had to be completed within 45 days of the next hearing, and that included the ultimate judgment.

Coincidentally, little was mentioned about Richard Smith, the leader of the after – school program, nor his involvement with Mark. That surprised Mark, given the fact that so much of his case was in connection with this man.

Meanwhile, Wayne and his team were working nonstop on Mark's case. Wayne knew that there was a missing link, and time was of the essence. The "black box" of survival, like its use after an airline disaster, would make all the difference.

"Bingo!" Wayne's investigator screamed upon realizing that he had hit the jackpot in unveiling the real facts of the case, and with no time to spare. The investigator and his partner went through documents involving the after – school program, and by following Smith, caught him meeting someone from a bank. It seemed as if cash was exchanged, and now, they had the pictures to prove it.

With some more research, the case came together, and they arranged to meet Wayne with their findings.

Wayne then called Mark. "Mark, your nightmares are over. Be here at six tonight."

CHAPTER 57

Mark got to Wayne's office, but did not feel as happy as Wayne's voice sounded over the phone. His day at the hearings made him apprehensive. If anything was a strategy for Mark, the union attorney quickly dismissed it.

"If you bring in evidence that ties to the case but is not a part of a speculation, then there is a good possibility that you will be brought up on additional charges. This is a new arbitrator, first learning about the education hearing procedures, so don't overburden her."

Would Wayne be able to represent Mark with all these guidelines and time restraints?

Mark had to be optimistic; he was reminded of Ellyn, who was happier than ever. He also thought of Melissa's full confidence in Wayne's work.

Wayne had a bright glow on his face, but Mark still was not convinced.

"Listen, I work to make my own money and reputation ... and I investigate for evidence and examine witnesses the way a real attorney should ... look at Ellyn.

Mark was convinced and started to listen to Wayne. In the little time Wayne had the case, he offered assurance to Mark that he would win the case and vindicate him from all charges and allegations – more than any union representation did in the months since Mark was charged.

"You would never guess what we found," and with no reaction from Mark, Wayne was concerned.

Then Mark proceeded to take out his notes and recall, detail by detail, the events of the first day of hearing and all the conversations surrounding it.

Wayne tried to interrupt Mark's monologue, but Mark kept talking.

"Are you going to let me do my job, or are you relying on some union idiot?" Wayne blurted out.

And then, there was silence.

"Thank you" Wayne continued. "Let's talk about the important stuff, as time and actions are of upmost importance."

Wayne then took over, and even when Mark tried to break into the conversation, he would not allow Mark the chance.

"What about my history of being a good teacher?"

"What I have is much more powerful than any teaching history or student records they never allow into the process anyway."

As it had turned out, document and money tampering had been going on within the school district for years. The Attorney General's office was trying to investigate the criminality of the missing money and false paperwork, yet union officials and politically connected people had successfully distracted the public from the truth.

Only when Wayne had paid informants for their tapes and records could people from the DOE, UFT, and private businesses be tied together. And, even better, Wayne was able to retrieve videos of meetings, including exchanges of cash.

Wayne had copies made and security placed on anything evidence that he needed. Additionally, as Wayne suspected that anyone involved in this case would be suspicious of anything going on, he placed the evidence under 24 – hour surveillance.

Sure enough, there were threats on tape, including guns and names.

It would be more than the Federal And State Government wanted, or had.

"You see, Mark, when your boss realized he gave you the paperwork, he did it deliberately so that a cover up would prevent any questioning of what was really going on. You were set up to 'accidentally' find the papers, and with your fingerprints on them, they had the proof they needed to say you were involved, that you tampered with the actual facts and then covered up all the money they took personally to use illegally." Smith played Mark, and everyone else ... even acted out like he knew nothing while he was alone ... just in case someone was watching ... like in security tapes."

Mark was speechless.

Wayne went on. "There's more. It seems that some of the parents and a teacher in the building were actually involved."

The question was: What was the next step, and when?

Wayne could not emphasize enough that Mark should keep this information to himself. "Try to avoid any contact with your union attorney. When is your next day to meet?"

"We have no date yet ... not that I know of ... anyway."

"Good, that means you won't be hearing anything within the next few days. Luckily, because of the time restrictions set for hearing and payment dates, we have time on our side."

They sat together, strategized, and by the end of the meeting, after phone calls and contacts, things were set in place.

CHAPTER 58

M elissa was entering an elevator to go up to see Wayne Gray just as Mark was taking the stairs down to exit.

Due to the timing and importance of information of both cases, Wayne realized he had no choice; he had to make them work together and build up momentum in order to have both settled to his satisfaction – complete vindication of both Mark and Melissa.

In all of his years of practicing education law, he never encountered such luck on his part. Two friends, college classmates, and both of them had been set up.

In all honesty, there had been times when Wayne felt that some of his education – oriented clients were somewhat guilty, especially those brought up on incompetency charges. But not Mark and Melissa.

Not everyone is geared to the profession that they choose, and that included educators. Some took courses, earned certificates, passed tests, but could not successfully execute their lessons in a meaningful way. Many people think that teachers have security through tenure; they have salaries, benefits, retirement packages, and are set for life. Too many, though, are simply average teachers, whether or not they spend hours preparing lessons and purchasing supplies or just go by the required union contracts and never add a penny or an ounce of effort more. They deserve to be fired. As in every other profession, there are those who act inappropriately and should be fired on the spot – not fined, not getting full salaries for years, and not having union protection because of who and what they knew within the system.

Mark and Melissa were different. They had glowing personnel files; they had founded and volunteered in all kinds of academic and social activities not just for their schools, but for the families and businesses in the communities in which each worked. For the most part, both led respectable lives outside their work. Neither had any criminal records, any suspicious activity surrounding them, and they came from good homes and had succeeded in a top 20 school in the heart of New York City.

And for those reasons, as well as the fact that within the past several days, evidence and witnesses were able to prove both to be innocent, Wayne knew that he had only one way to go: soon and fast.

CHAPTER 59

The stage was set. The lights were bright in some spots and dimmed in others. Chairs were neatly organized in rows, as were the assorted soft drinks and bottled waters on the corner refreshment table. Press kits and headshots of Mark, Melissa, and Wayne were neatly piled in stacks, and throughout the room were pens, note pads, and copies of the speech that Wayne was about to give.

Wayne invited Michael and Ellyn to sit front row and watch what he called "live theater."

Reporters, bloggers, invited guests, and some people who had realized the seriousness of what was about to take place began to enter the large building nearly an hour before the scheduled time.

All of the important characters also arrived, including Melissa and her family, Mark and Sarah, and their families, Benjamin Bronstein, Ellyn and Michael, and many staff within the DOE, including the assistant to the Chancellor and the Deputy Mayor. That was a surprise, and when Wayne caught a glimpse of her standing in the corner by the refreshments, he made a bee line over to reintroduce himself, since they had met in the past at several political and business functions.

Wayne knew this was a significant moment in his career. He had to play it wisely and safely. He also liked Ellyn, Mark, and Melissa, and wanted them vindicated in a timely and positive manner.

He went into his private bathroom, fixed his tie, brushed his hair and teeth, and reviewed his notes. He made several changes and decided to keep his words simple and brief. The points would come across in just a short amount of time.

Wayne's associates gathered everyone together, and introduced him. The room was silent; it would be possible to hear a pin drop. Those from the DOE sat together, as if they had a plan of their own. The group distracted Wayne momentarily, for he knew evidence and witnesses could not win over rhetoric.

Wayne stepped up to the podium. There was not a single sound, not even a pencil swirl; all eyes and ears were on him. He looked directly into the eyes of the Deputy Mayor and knew exactly what they were thinking: trouble.

"Ladies and Gentleman, members of the press, fellow concerned taxpayers, guests from the Department of Education, our special guest, the Deputy Mayor of the great city of New York, colleagues, and esteemed professionals in all areas of education, I am so glad to invite you here today." At that point, Wayne asked Ms. Deputy Mayor to stand and wave to all.

She respectfully stood momentarily, wanting to hide.

Wayne changed the next few sentences and spoke "off the cuff." "We in New York have the best education system in place," he said, knowing that everyone in that room had the facts to prove otherwise, yet he knew he had to eventually work with all of the guests, and on future cases.

"Unfortunately, when you send a bushel of apples to a supermarket, there are always a few that start out damaged, or suddenly turn rotten for whatever reason, like a climate control, its surroundings, the variety of characters around it … you get the point."

"Ultimately, those few bad apples give the rest of the bunch a bad image, to the point that, by reputation of a grocer or a buyer, an entire selection of apples is thrown out, even those that were perfectly delicious, ones where one bite gave you such a satisfaction that you didn't have to call the doctor or grab that chocolate cake not on your diet."

A few members of the audience laughed, for they could relate. Wayne took the time to sip some water, to keep his voice clear and loud.

He went off the papers and spoke from his heart for a minute, deciding to introduce Ellyn and briefly review her case as an opening to what was about to happen next.

By then, most of the Department of Education and government employees knew what was coming and dreaded the next words, while some reporters were quickly Googling Ellyn and Michael and found out almost immediately.

The Deputy Mayor turned to her school liaison and gave a look of defeat.

"It is with great sadness that, after sharing with you the experiences and circumstances surrounding the harassment, for lack of a better word, of an excellent teacher, Ellyn Marks. I had hoped that would have been the last time I saw such injustice. I am standing before you today angry, very angry. I am angry that I have to share being a part of a system that hurts every one of us. Each one of us, and even you, Ms. Deputy Mayor," Wayne purposely made a point of mentioning her, directing cameras and recorders on her to catch her initial reaction before her "professionalism" kicked in, "You and I work hard minute after minute, hour after hour, day after day, so that we can put bread on the table, clothes on our families' backs, and give our children a better life and more opportunity than we ever had, and what our parents and grandparents came to this country for, education and opportunity ..."

Wayne stopped for a moment to wipe his eye, as if he were wiping away a tear.

"We strive each and every day for simple things, never taking them for granted, like the eggs and milk that we purchase, the gas we need for our vehicles, the libraries that house books written hundreds of years ago that relate to our emotions and lifestyles this very day."

Wayne took another breath, playing out what he had practiced in his lessons of lecturing and presenting.

"Ladies and Gentleman, I cannot wait any longer. Mark Ollins and Melissa Dobbs, please join me by the podium." Wayne introduced Mark first. "Mark graduated with honors from New York University, and could have easily worked within a highly successful family business or accepted the multiple business opportunities thrown at him. Instead, he chose – against the wishes of many around him – a career in education, going for advanced degrees, spending thousands on education, school supplies, volunteering time, money, and effort to a cause he believed in, helping children, children who did not have the chances he had in life. He had support from family and friends that surrounded him daily. Mark has won awards, organized tutoring, and garnered love and respect not just from his students, but from co – workers, his own union staff, businesses, and families within this school neighborhood. What was his reward? Mark was set up in a scandal that cost you and me a lot of money, and I am going to make sure that, when this investigation is done publicly and correctly, you will see how furious that I am, not only for what has happened unfairly to one of public school's best educators, but as a taxpayer, as are all of you. Again, remember this situation involves your own hard – earned dollars, and a man being falsely accused, publicly, professionally, and personally humiliated. Most importantly, it involves hurting innocent young children who benefit from daily contact and guidance from this man.

"The Department of Education of the great City of New York, and many others with great influence, power, and money to spend – again, your money – would like you to believe that this successful educator and businessman is a crook, a fraud, a liar, and one who should not be teaching your children, or working with your friends and neighbors. A lot of your money, and many people putting in all sorts of hours and creativity have gone about intentionally setting up this humanitarian and decent human being to 'cover up,' for lack of a better phrase, what can only be factually witnessed as criminal activities. Please turn your attention to the screen."

Wayne's assistants showed the audience a tape with a clear audio describing in detail an exchange of funds, falsification of documents, and even manipulation of Mark's after – school superior to arrange a setup. On the tape, the superior was shown on several occasions being in questionable places and discussing things that were definitely out – of – line.

The film stopped there. As the audience sat in disbelief, several staff members from Wayne's offices handed copies of documents with both falsified signatures and information and other documents containing the actual facts that Wayne was able to obtain within hours before this meeting and share to compare.

"It's time for the appropriate agencies and public officials to handle this case. But first and foremost, I am here to publicly vindicate Mark, and I feel quite confident that all those involved need to clear him well within an appropriate amount of time, with a clear past and present professional record."

"And now, here stands Melissa Dobbs, another educator recognized by co – workers, parents and most of all the children who look up to her and lean on her for so many things more than a lesson or grade."

Wayne played on his audience's emotions once again. He took a deep breath, and sighed in a facial expression of disbelief.

"Most women during this late stage of pregnancy are eagerly awaiting the birth of their child." He stopped for a few moments. "Ladies and gentleman, listen carefully, for what I am about to say will shock you, even put you in a spin. I simply cannot make these facts up. The wonderful Department of Education and all the connected agencies involved in investigations would like you to believe that Melissa is a lonely, sad, 'loose' woman. She excelled in her student teaching position so much so that the administrators in her first public school experience actually stole her work and privately profited from selling her lesson plans and teaching tools online. Witnesses came forward and visited these offices to sign affidavits. Each document confirms her suspicions of months ago, after Melissa's story went public at the school she is currently assigned to."

The audience awed in union.

"Melissa felt she couldn't do anything and simply transferred to a school where parents, co – workers, and most importantly, students, loved and adored her. Again, Melissa devoted her all, and her students excelled despite all the hardships and adversities they faced daily. And how was she rewarded? She was drugged and raped, and thus became pregnant, by not one, but two school employees."

For a few moments the room burst into a shocked hubbub, with shouted questions from the press representatives, until Wayne used his arms to plead for quiet.

"I know this is a shocking charge," Wayne continued, but a check of police reports will reveal that this afternoon, based on the sworn statement of a school custodian and," Wayne stressed, "DNA evidence provided by a blanket used in the event and saved and stored away by the custodian who came forward, not only the custodian but an assistant principal were arrested on multiple charges arising from that rape."

Once again, the listeners in the room could not hold back their shocked reactions and heavy emotions; Wayne waited for the conflicting voices and questions to subside.

In that pause, Melissa felt a sharp pain.

CHAPTER 60

Within minutes, Melissa's pain turned to agony. She sank to the floor and started to scream.

"Someone call 9 – 1 – 1!" several people yelled simultaneously; her parents, Michael, and others tried to kneel to help her.

Michael observed that she was in labor. The baby might have been a few weeks early, but Melissa seemed ready to give birth.

Before Wayne was able to finish the conference, all the press and guests became obviously sidetracked. Wayne was just about to share the most disgusting, yet most important, part of his "event."

After a few minutes, Melissa was removed, and Wayne and his staff tried to return some order to the event. After all, they had all come for a purpose. However, many were so overwhelmed with what was happening with Melissa that the press conference ended in a state of confusion.

"My offices will offer any and all assistance to all who are working for justice prevailing," Wayne concluded.

With that, many left, and Wayne went immediately into his office, locked his doors, and called Melissa's parents.

Melissa had just arrived into the emergency room and more than half-way dilated. She would be giving birth shortly.

The next morning, as the sun rose brightly through her hospital window, Melissa pushed hard, and harder, for nearly half an hour until a six – pound baby boy came into the world.

Melissa gazed at her son lovingly, and held him tightly. She kissed his head and promised him a life filled with love, trust and friends. It was something that her own grandfather said to her many, many years before.

Her OB – GYN reminded Melissa that she needed her rest, but she simply could not take her mind off of the conference, and how Wayne was about to save her life.

Her parents, cousins, Ellyn, Mark, and Michael were all waiting to meet the baby and to check in on Melissa.

Her parents went in first. They hugged and kissed her, and the nurse brought the baby in for its first feeding. Melissa and the baby took to breast feeding right away.

They walked out and told the crowd how gorgeous the baby was. It was as if the last few months had never happened.

Not a word was said about the press event.

About fifteen minutes later, the nurse walked out of Melissa's room and told the crowd they could see her, but suggested that guests go in only two at a time. She walked away and the entire group snuck in. They simply could not wait.

Melissa sat up. "Did I ruin the press event? Wayne will kill me."

They all laughed. Mark's cell phone rang. It was Wayne. He wanted to know what had happened, and Mark handed Melissa the phone. Wayne congratulated her, then asked her to give the cell phone back to Mark.

Mark put him on speaker, and although not all could hear and Wayne's words did not come out totally clear, everyone heard the summary.

Wayne told him that he had received a personal call from the Mayor, who said that he would like Wayne to work with his staff personally to investigate all the corruption that he discovered, and that he would like to help vindicate all those who were clearly innocent, and proceed with criminal charges against those who broke laws.

Wayne was skeptical about the call, but told the room that everything would be taken care of in a speedy manner. The public knew everything, the media knew everything, and the public system would have to spin itself out of a very tangled web that even Sir Walter Scott could not begin to unwind.

Melissa asked her mother to call Wayne back.

"Mom, Dad, don't go ... I want you to listen."

"Wayne, you saved my life and gave my son hope for a great future; it's time that he is given a name, a name that represents trust, honor, and respect." Melissa stopped, "Wayne, would it be OK with you if I named my son Wayne Michael? Wayne after you, and Michael after my Grandfather, who would have loved to have met this little bundle, and always told me to get a good education and make a better life for myself with opportunities he didn't have."

Wayne was touched and, of course, responded with joy and pride. "When I can meet my namesake?"

Melissa's visitors left to let her get rest. Melissa never felt better, and was determined to move on with her life positively, worked to gain strength for the trip home. Her parents insisted on taking both Melissa and baby Wayne to their home, where they had set up the guest room as a nursery.

Wayne, Ellyn, Michael, Mark, and Sarah all visited Melissa and baby Wayne.

When Sarah and Mark returned to their own apartment after seeing Melissa, baby Wayne, and her family, Sarah looked directly into Mark's eyes.

"How did you feel seeing the baby?"

"I just can't believe a baby came out of all of this."

Standing next to Mark in the small kitchen, Sarah responded, "Not one baby, but two."

CHAPTER 61

Within the next few weeks, Mark and Melissa were cleared of all charges and asked to return to their classrooms.

Wayne met with several associates who worked directly with the Mayor's office, first to thank him, and then to gather what evidence they could in working on their investigations.

Wayne trusted them to a point, but made sure that everything was done to help Melissa and Mark. Now, it seemed like every employee who was wronged, and every media outlet, wanted to work with Wayne.

He hired more staff and won and settled many more cases for those that he felt needed justice.

Wayne Gray turned down cases where he felt terminations were justified, cases in which no one was harassed, humiliated, and attacked.

Ellyn, Mark, and Melissa never returned to a classroom, despite all types of offers, from charter, private, and even higher education institutions. The memories of scandal had taken their toll. The biggest losers were the hundreds of potentials, students, and their families that lost out of having them as an educator and friend.

Melissa started dating one of Michael's cousins, an oral surgeon who loved little Wayne as if he were his own. Melissa returned to her apartment and started a tutoring service, adjusting hours to accommodate the baby's needs. She lost the weight that she had gained in previous months, and then some; Melissa changed her hair and dress styles and made many friends within her new apartment complex. She never thought that she could be happy. Because of the rape and the baby, Melissa was able to secure damages from the city for five million dollars as well as maintain all her benefits and pension. She never spoke publicly about the incident, nor did she ever look back.

Mark worked solely on his various ventures, made more money and worked less. Sarah stopped working as they looked for homes in Westchester, New York, and Connecticut.

Best of all, nine months after Wayne Michael was born, Mark and Sarah gave him a wonderful gift, a friend. Little Michael was born, and a party celebrating all the family was held in the country club that Mark had grown up with. Ellyn, Melissa and Mark made the point of creating a photo image similar to the one they took on graduation days all those years ago.

From three New York University collegiate students through different paths, Ellyn, Mark, and Melissa finally found peace and each other and shared an experience many cannot relate to.

Everything You Need To Know and Ask About The Education System

This is our non fiction section addressing areas of interest to anyone involved in the education system and that includes you.

Many questions will be asked it is your job to investigate fully an answer don't trust an "expert" or source simply because they claim to be an authority. Compare more than one reference and more than one professional.

We are practicing logical reasoning something we expect our students yes, even those in the lower elementary grades, to practice in everyday routines and tasks. Think as you read if a question or some of the information overlaps and where and why.

Take notes, add your thoughts and start discussions to see what first reactions you receive.

Obviously, this is not a dictionary, encyclopedia (do they use them anymore?) Or Google. Just because I define something based on my research does not mean you agree or it is really accurate although all the information in this section was compiled from print based documentation.

Again, this area has nothing to do with me personally these are questions every taxpayer, mother, educator, textbook publisher, food service supplier and others should think about as they bring family members into this system.

After each group of questions there will be some space to take notes. Make sure you have your pens, pencils, highlighters and post its as you read ...

OPINIONS

How much do you really know about "education" of any type?

How do you define "education"? If education is a process of receiving or imparting information, then aren't we all educators and students routinely? What makes the education system unique?

As it says in the Talmud, "He who teaches a child is like one who writes on paper; but one who teaches old people is like one who writes on blotted paper." What does that actually mean and how can we relate this quote with logic and reason to our own education values?

Where do you get your information about education to figure out your opinions? Are they always accurate? Do they represent a bias? Are there underlying goals as to who and what is being shared?

Is the education system in the United States a success? Is it a failure? What information do I have to back up my statement?

Do we spend enough money in our country on education? Does our nation neglect the education system in their budgets? Do I (the reader) know how much money is actually spent on education as part of an entire federal/state/local budget?

Who pays for education? Is this a simple answer? Does "pay" involve money only?

Is education a right or a privilege?

Can anyone become a teacher? Principal?

If you are a good guardian, does that make you a good educator?

Do parents have enough input into the school system?

Should education laws change as our status as the number one world power is being challenged?

HISTORY OF EDUCATION

How did formal education begin? Where/Why/Who/When/What were connected to the origins of formal education?

Who are the real champions of education? What were their achievements?

Who are the foes of the concept of learning? Why – and what are their concerns about an education system?

What does separation of church and state actually mean?

Should public school buildings be used for church choirs? Religious assemblies?

Who decides a school calendar? Is it a fair calendar?

Does time in a school building qualify as the only education needed?

Here are some highlights of our history that correlate to the history of education. When the pilgrims settled here, their education contained mostly religious ideas since they were free to practice their beliefs here. In 1636, Harvard College opens in Massachusetts. In 1642, Massachusetts Bay School Law is passed, which seems to be the first official education law. It establishes the first curriculum; ensuring children know religion and the capital laws of where they live.

In 1647, the Massachusetts Law established that in every town of at least 50 families hire a teacher and educate how to read and write. If towns had more than 100 families, Latin was also required. In 1751, Benjamin Franklin opens in Philadelphia an Academy that includes courses in history, navigation, and classical languages.

In 1779, Thomas Jefferson established a system with learning for those who are educated and those you work hard – labor. The blackboard was invented in 1801 by James Pillans. During the 1800s, the first "teachers

– education" school opens, schools start to be run by superintendents and children with learning disabilities are funded. The National Teachers Association opens in Philadelphia in 1857.

In 1867, the Department of Education was created with the purpose of building a solid school system. It has gone through many changes, including those in 1979, which still are being used, expanded and criticized today.

As we enter the 1900s, we saw starting to see the foundations of education as we define it today. In 1917, the Smith – Hughes Act provides federal funding for vocational education in connection to assembly – line manufacturing skills. In 1948, the Educational Testing Service is formed and committees and examinations are merging throughout the nation. In the late 1970s, legislation in states including Massachusetts and California freeze property taxes and thus ties to public schools.

As we look into education today, many questions arise daily about each and every aspect of education and how it ties to other aspects of our lives regardless of where you live, your lifestyle, your economic conditions and your future.

Questions/Debates Relating to History of Education

Which countries continue to rate the best in their education systems? Why? How are they run?

Which countries seem to have the have the most failure or successful education? Why?

Is education required in all countries?

Does education worldwide help our economy or hurt it?

What patterns do we see successful in other countries education systems? Which patterns fail? Why?

Do you know the history of education in our country?

How does our education system compare to worldwide education?

What was the original purpose of creating a Department of Education? Are they still the same? There are thousands of pages written about the department's history, growth and the debates of its success and failures. There is simply too much information for me to share here. You research, again, use your logic and think about using the pros and improving the cons.

What are some of the most important federal laws and why?

Who are "educational lobbyists?"

Do you know how officials on a local, state and federal level vote in relation to any education issue?

Should English be taught in the United States as the primary language?

How should the Social Studies curriculum be taught today in the United States? Is factually correct history being taught? Who decided what constitutes history?

Who decides where schools are located and what type of buildings are constructed and how they are used?

Should public and charter schools share physical building sites?

Should private homes be used as schools?

How is success in education measured?

RELATED TO EDUCATION
KEY WORDS AND TOPICS

How were the systems of public and private education devised?

What is homeschooling? What is the history of it? Is it a success or failure? Why? Is homeschooling today like what we see in the images of movies and television shows like "Little House On the Prairie?"

Where can we find out more about homeschooling and which people work on their behalf?

The largest homeschooling organization seems to be the Home School Legal Defense Association. It is a nonprofit advocacy organization established to defend and advance the constitutional right of parents. Through annual memberships, HSLDA helps tens of thousands of families united in service together, providing a strong voice when and where needed.

Who helps homeschooling parents decide what their children should learn and how do they get their materials? Does the age of internet and computer information sharing help homeschooling? How do children develop social and interaction skills?

What is a curriculum? Are all curriculums the same? Who should decide what is in a curriculum?

A universal definition of curriculum is a group of courses and subjects taught within an educational institution. By defining curriculum this way, we are begging the following debates open for discussion – Does all curriculum have to be carefully planned? Who decides what is taught on a universal level – or should topic information be decided by continent, country, state, or region? Should a universal organization like the United Nations have final say in a curriculum?

What is early childhood education? Universal Pre–K? How do they compare? Differ?

Children as early as four – years – old are now being offered schooling. Universal Pre–K advocates are in favor of accessibility to all children worldwide.

What is "classroom management?" Who should be accountable for it?

Classroom management is engaging students in a most positive, comfortable, yet engaging and organized environment. Most educators agree that the best scenario includes a student's ability to achieve social and academic skills. What most agree also enhances discipline and academic achievement are the issues of the family and community a student is surrounded and influenced by. Who is accountable for the success and/ or failure of classroom management is always questioned based on the demographics and political state at the time of discussion.

Who should control a "school climate?" Is it always controllable? What factors in and out of a school classroom, lunchroom, building and outside grounds effect the "climate?"

What is 'brain – based" learning?

Brain – based learning applies to each and every one of us. We are learning through teaching methods, experiences as adults, and how lessons are created and executed. Our brain works differently as we grow, where we live, our social preferences and our emotions.

What are "multiple intelligences?"

Every educator learns about Professor Howard Gardner's seven multiple intelligences. There is a lot written about his theory and I suggest you look further into it – and see which intelligences you relate to the most.

Do the theories of "brain – based learning" and multiple intelligence's relate? You decide after you find out more about both.

I remember learning (in one of my education courses) how I am a visual learner. Because I am aware of this, I always position myself in a spot in a gym class, in a course where I am learning a skill or even in a food store the in best position to see. I "eat with my eyes." Think about your five senses and where you learn best – can you do your best work hearing, what about memorizing to note taking – all tied to our brain – based learning skills.

Who are "mentors?" To correctly define a mentor is someone who assists another person with less knowledge facts, expertise and advice. In schools, we relate mentoring to helping both students and staff in different ways. Students receive extra help in many courses both within a school building and privately. Staff receive mentoring help through professional development programs and budgets arranged through education systems and unions.

What is a "whole child" learning program?

"Whole child" learning includes academic instruction, safety, a physically and emotionally healthy situation for a student. Many health and education organizations work together on public awareness and public policies. Check out which groups work within your neighborhoods.

How do technology and computers play into classrooms presently and in the future?

What is all the controversy about math and science scores? There is so much information available to learn and compare. Take the time to investigate graphs and charts and compare worldwide education success rates in these areas regarding grades, jobs and country/state economies. Is the United States lagging in teaching math and science as we are prone to believe?

What "tools" are needed for quality education? Who decides what textbooks are used?

What is "higher education?"

We relate colleges and universities to "higher education" as we receive degrees of choice for eventual employment opportunities. Yet as this book is published, we find much debate over these institutions and what is taught.

What is a degree? Why do people need degrees? How many degrees do people actually need?

What are "trade schools?" Once a popular choice to garner an education and assist in employment opportunities – are they something our country needs to revisit and update?

What are charter schools? Charter schools are the subject of so many articles, documentaries and tied to so many other policy topics that I will let you define them as you will? Do they work? Is this type of school just a trend? Are any charter schools failing? If so, they why?

What is "leveled reading?"

Do you hear the term leveled reading alphabet, leveled library, book – bags or bundles, and correlation charts? These all relate to the idea that each student reads on an individual letter level, according to their abilities of both pronounce the words and pause according to punctuation and then understanding what they are reading and connecting it to their personal experiences.

The debate here is whether a student can benefit from this system, when so much is dependent on their personal abilities and support from home?

What is "fuzzy math?"

Started in 1965 "fuzzy math" combines theories of using mathematics and logic. It does not depend on rote learning and memorizing facts. There is much debate today as to its success and if "fuzzy math" works best with some concrete facts. There are many who blame the success or failure of Common Core math to "fuzzy math."

How many hours/days/weeks/months should be required for education within a school building?

Does all "schooling" need to be in a contained environment?

Does class size matter? What ratio is a successful student to educator in class? Should every class have aides? Paraprofessionals?

Who are paraprofessionals and what are their official duties?

Who are school aides?

Who are school volunteers? Should they be forced to follow the same guidelines as paid staff?

Who are school safety officers? How do their jobs work in connection to police officers, police policies and in relation to precincts?

What is the Leadership Academy and its association in the New York City Department of Education? Does it properly train our supervisors?

What is Teacher's College as part of Columbia University? Does it properly train our educators?

EVALUATIONS

What are evaluations as they relate to education? Are you aware that school systems, districts, principals and even communities surrounding schools undergo all types of testing and evaluations? The topic to debate today seems to be evaluating students and connecting their grades to a teacher's effectiveness.

ARE EVALUATIONS FAIR OR UNFAIR?

How are you evaluated at your job? How you decide which professionals to use for your health or which goods to purchase? If your doctor or lawyer does not want you as a client, can they drop you? If Macy's gives you a better sale for the exact same product as Bloomingdales, where would you purchase it?

Should you evaluate a teacher, principal, school and its community the same way? Should a school community judge its parents and students the same way?

Are all surveys completed by students, parents, staff and community residents answered without a bias all the time? Should educators in a private school or a rural building be judged the same as a school or teacher in a district filled with students that live in underprivileged areas?

Teachers prepare for their occupation in courses that cost thousands of dollars and can take years to complete degrees. Most are extremely competent, reliable and trustworthy. They work well beyond the requirements of their contracts and spend many more hours and dollars on making sure the future of their students have a good foundation for a solid future. You decide, should their future employment be based on one test?

COMMON CORE

The Common Core is a set of high – quality academic standards in mathematics and English Language Arts/literacy (ELA). These learning goals outline what a student should know and be able to do at the end of each grade.

Common Core creators have defined literacy, themes, literary texts, narrative writing and fluency to combine logical reasoning, but in order to succeed, one needs to know and practice simple punctuation, grammar and command of the English language. Seems like the same happens within the math area. Solving simple math problems, because of the way they are presented to a student becomes a skill of combining several logical explanations. Steps that include estimating, rounding, comparing and checking often take away thought from the actual problem, thus confusing the student who not only gives a wrong answer, but does not complete a problem at all in a timely fashion.

Parents and guardians who were not "trained" in these skills cannot help their child to understand and complete homework assignments or prepare for tests.

Common Core is a term so commonly used, yet it is rarely defined and/or understood. While many agree that common core in ideology might seem reasonable if practiced correctly, there are definite issues as to its execution from school to school and its evaluation. Is it fair to evaluate a teacher or school based so much on a single test when we don't know if the school supplies all the needed resources, the teachers understand and are uniform in its teaching and if students are using these skills at home and with parent support. Do parents even know how to assist their children and offer them guidance and work with their educators?

Race To The Top

Race to the Top was announced by President Barack Obama in 2009 as a federal funded program as part of the American Recovery and Re-investment Act. The program was created for grades K – 12 rewarding updating reforms and innovations. It seems if you read more on the program, schools were to "turn – around" from poor functioning to grade – level achieving and higher. As of 2015, published reports "claim" to have dedicated over $4 billion federal dollars to over 22 million students in mostly low – income schools.

Multi – Culturalism

What is multiculturalism? How does it relate to education worldwide and in the United States?

Multicultural education is a process that permeates all aspects of school practices, policies and organization as a means to ensure the highest levels of academic achievement for all students. It helps students develop a positive self – concept by providing knowledge about the histories, cultures, and contributions of diverse groups. It prepares all students to work actively toward structural equality in organizations and institutions by providing the knowledge, dispositions, and skills for the redistribution of power and income among diverse groups.

The National Association for Multicultural Education is located in Washington D.C. and addresses the issues tied to the ideas of equity, inclusion, diversity and justice within the education system.

Much has been written about multiculturalism. Multiculturalism education has been the subject of recent speeches and articles of world leaders as it relates to worldwide current events. It appears that some world leaders in Europe, North America and Australia question the value of multicultural education because even as it teaches tolerance and inclusion, acts of violence are spreading and seem more vicious than ever before.

One of the first to question the pros and cons of multicultural education is German Chancellor Angela Merkel, and as early as October 2010. It has been reported that she stated that German multiculturalism has failed – that more Germans felt that Germany was being taken over by foreigners and that it did not help the education and employment issues facing the country. In 2014, British Prime Minister David Cameron spoke against multicultural education because he sees different cultures living separate lives and not united in a common community. As more terrorist organizations arise and more outlets are using to recruit, various policy makers are looking at the benefits or deficiencies of multicultural education as part of an entire society in regard to long – term results.

Names Related to Education Past and Present

Ella Flagg Young

First Female Superintendent in Chicago and later National Education Association President

John Dewey and his daughter **Evelyn**

Authors and Promotors of progressive education practices

Charlotte Hawkins Brown

Educator and Founder of the Palmer Memorial Institute Trailblazer for African – American excellence in education

Lucy Spaque Mitchell

Founder, Bureau of Educational Experiments Center that studies child development and learning abilities

Lewis Madison Terman

Psychologist and Educator that studied "gifted" children

Benjamin Bloom

Did you ever hear the term "Bloom's Taxonomy?" Bloom is the primary author of a handbook specifying the six levels of cognitive domain. It is still used and referred to today.

Albert Shanker

One of the founders and former president of United Federation of Teachers Former president of American Federation of Teaches

Sandra Feldman

Former President of both AFT and UFT

Randi Weingarten

Current President of American Federation of Teachers, Former President of United Federation of Teachers

Geoffrey Canada

CEO, Harlem Children's Zone Promise Academy

Michelle Rhee

Former Chancellor of Washington, D.C. public schools

Founder of StudentsFirst – advocates education reform, Author

Michael Bloomberg

Former Mayor of NYC that won mayoral control of school system

Eva Moskowitz

Former Council member in New York City

Founder and CEO of Success Academy Charter Schools

Wendy Kopp

Founder, Teach for America, Author

Jason Bedrick

Policy Analyst, Cato's Institute Center for Educational Freedom

There are thousands we could list and identify. Do you have an area of interest to learn about? Check out the names associated with that topic. It seems as if the current trend is identifying non – educators who have in the past and currently engage in the education process through their work, dedication and financial abilities. Names like Helen Keller, Thurgood Marshall, Bill Gates, and Mark Zuckerberg are always related to education topics.

Parents/Guardians

What are the rights of parents?

What are the obligations of parents?

How many parents actually participate in school activities? What percentage in each school?

Should parents be held accountable for student behavior? Academic skills?

Should parents be graded on report cards?

Is there a way to fairly evaluate a parent or guardian? Should we?

Who are "tiger moms?"

Has the change in the "makeup" of a family affected schooling?

Should a school community know the backgrounds of parents convicted of crimes like rape, robbery and murder or anything that deals with safety?

What is "opt out?"

Should parents/guardians expect to have access to educators on a 24/7 basis?

Should parents expect educators to act as social workers? Babysitters? Nurses? Any other occupations other that of being a teacher/principal or aide?

Should educators be more active in their own families' school activities and help run Parent Teacher Associations because of their professional knowledge?

STUDENTS

What are student's rights?

What are student obligations within a school system?

Should students be allowed to be a part of a social promotion program?

Are all students created equal?

Should students be a part of an affirmative action program when applying for schools? Monies? Grants?

Should students who continually misbehave and break regulations always be allowed to attend a school? When is enough – actually enough?

Should students be required to wear uniforms?

Should students be given all supplies, including computers and expensive equipment?

Should students be allowed to carry and use electronic devices like cell phones and computers in school? Has the use of the equipment promoted better learning?

What involves student bullying? Can students get in trouble for bullying a classmate off of school grounds with school punishments?

How should students be evaluated? Should all students be evaluated exactly the same?

What is a pass? What is a fail?

Who provides student transportation? Should a student have a choice of schools as it relates to the choice of transportation and commuting time?

What is a good learning environment?

When should students "opt out" of classes and/or testing? If they "Opt Out" who should be in charge of their accountability?

A group called the Pacific Education Group, a San Francisco – based organization, tries to help public schools deal with achievement and disciplinary issues involving minority students. It's goal is teaching staff how to treat minorities differently? Does this help or hurt the student in the long run? Should taxpayers be responsible for paying for such a program?

Special Education/School Services

What services are required by law in school systems?

Should all special needs cases be treated equally?

What is an IEP? Does your student have an IEP? An Individualized Education Program is a written document designed for an individual to address whether a student qualifies for services and to keep track of progress.

Do these laws apply in public/private/other schooling environments?

Are schools supposed to supply meals? Medical needs? Material goods?

Should schools supply all the supplies, regardless of actual use, finances and benefits to current teaching?

Should schools pay for trips to cultural events? What about carnivals, parties, proms, and social programs?

Unions

What are unions?

How did unions begin and why?

When did the education system start unionizing? Why did they unionize?

How many unions are involved in the education system? For example, did you know vendors are involved in unions – so are school safety officers?

Are unions powerful?

What is tenure?

What kind of benefits do union members get as part of their belonging to a union?

Union members pay dues. What benefits do members receive as a member of the union?

What are the connections with unions and political leaders?

What is the AFT – The American Federation of Teachers?

What is the UFT – The United Federation of Teachers?

What is NYSUT – The New York State Union of Teachers?

How are teachers unions the same? How do they differ?

What is CSA? It is the Counsel of School Supervisors and Administrators – the union in New York City. How are they like the UFT? How do they differ? When do they work together? Should they join forces with other government unions like the police and firefighters unions? When should they all fight separate issues?

What are union "protections" in contracts?

What are the steps required by law to file grievances? Are they successful?

What is a 3020a hearing? What leads a teacher to a hearing regarding incompetency and or misconduct?

What is a "rubber room?" Believe it or not, I have actually heard people say they think they are rooms teachers are put in with walls covered with rubber. Are you aware that principals, supervisors and other school employees can be assigned a "rubber room" location to wait pending the outcome of an investigation?

Who is an arbitrator? How do his/her responsibilities compare to a judge? How much do they get paid? Who pays them?

What is COPE? Do you know how much money each teacher pays to COPE? COPE stands for the Committee on Political Education and is part of UFT's political action work. The money raised is used to lobby on city, state and federal levels. Most educators don't even realize that money is automatically taken from their paychecks and given to political candidates they may not even agree with – on issues not related to education. Do all educator unions have similar lobbying groups in their states?

CONTRACTS

How many of you actually would be able to read the entire Obamacare legislation and understand it? How many think your elected officials – who voted on it and don't follow it, yet forced you into it – really read it? In fact, we know the answer from their own remarks.

The same holds true for the entire teacher's contract, supervisors contract and any union contract that deals with the education system – even a contract for supplying food or cleaning services. Did you ever hear the term "Quantity vs Quality?" Each contract is so wordy and carefully worded, yet loopholes can be found in each to somehow confuse an average person.

The United Federation of Teachers in New York City is a perfect contract to research and read. It is online. It is also available in print, as an actual booklet, divided into categories and sub – categories that add up to many, many pages. Time after time, contracts run out and teachers perform duties with outdated information. According to the contract, some of the most frequently researched areas include pay and benefits, teacher evaluations, paperwork and lessons, actual workday requirements, teaching curriculum, and the status of seniority and ATRs – which are teachers who are in a substitution pool in the case where a school has downsized or closed. Sections of the contract include DOE documents.

But what the contract doesn't answer – is it really a uniform system? What goes on behind closed doors in verbal agreements? What happens when staff members are treated differently as well as school buildings in surveys and reviews because of personal relationships with influential figures and historic reputation? Are all school grades really fair?

The New York State United Teachers Association contract is also online. Many of their sections discuss research and education, legislative actions and social justice and services. If you are a government official that disagrees with them, what happens.

Wisconsin is a state that should be researched. Act 10 in the teachers contracts has been the focal point of many legal and public battles. You can find the entire contact and coverage of it online.

When a teacher is disciplined, the New York State Law is called 3020 – a Code of Disciplinary Procedures and Penalties. Again the actual law is many, many pages. I suggest you research and look at the actual documentation and see if you understand it? Share it with others, including those you feel are well – educated and business oriented, and share your thoughts.

Media – Books/Movies/ Blogs/Publications

Columnists and Media Coverage

Depending on the writer, editorial and publisher personal feelings and bias – education media information can be discussed and distributed in a variety of ways that might not always seems realistic and truthful. A great example of this is how a teacher that is "innocent until proven guilty" in a court of law is portrayed before an outcome. Would you, who could possibly be going through the same turmoil, want a trial by media? What about two consenting adults having a relationship during their personal time? How many office affairs did the television show "Mad Men" entertain us with? Or writing a comment on a personal Facebook or Twitter account? Should teachers be treated any differently than any other professionals?

Almost every major daily print outlet has assigned writers and pays syndicated columnists to cover education and issues related to the system. It would be best for you to research some of the newspapers in the biggest urban areas and the smaller rural lands and compare articles, photos and editorials. It would also be a good idea to read some reader responses and letters.

The Education Action Group is an organization whose specific goal is to get news out about education in traditional outlets and social media. Articles involve parents, staff, students and events involving schools.

Here are some names of reporters and printed outlets covering education routinely I suggest researching ...

In New York, The Post seems to have the most coverage. Yoav Gonen and Aaron Short seem to byline the most articles on education. Columnists Andrea Peyser and Michael Goodwin write a lot about education as well. So do the political columnists as issues overlap.

Jay Mathews writes articles for the Washington Post. There are other reporters at the Washington Post that also have twitter accounts. They include Nick Anderson, Lyndsey Layton, Jenna Johnson, who writes about higher education as a blogger for Campus Overload, and Valerie Strauss, who also runs The Answer Sheet blog.

Tamar Lewin writes for The New York Times. Curtis Morgan is the Education Editor for the Miami Herald and Greg Toppo and Mary Beth Marklein write for USA Today.

Magazines like TIME and Newsweek report on education, along with many newspapers and magazines devoted just to education.

BLOGS

There are hundreds of blogs, twitter accounts and other social media outlets dedicated to education issues as a whole or dedicated to one area of expertise. Here are just a few I have heard about or seen as they seem to be some of the more known ones. Again, pick a topic and research it through social media and compare the issues versus the opinions of those writing and sharing the information.

Betsy Combier – parent advocates.org and nycrubberroomreporter. blogspot.com

Francesco Portelos – nyc teacher – Portelos has written and is the subject of many reporters articles and news stories about his tenure as a teacher for the NYCDOE

dianeravitch.com – education blog

www.teachthought.com

features over 50 education blogs for students/parents/educators to use

There seems to be to date over 20 blogs devoted to administration and principals.

Two of the most followed are connected principals.com and The Principal's office.com.

For Special Education needs, again there are many blogs, and within this topic there are subareas devoted to students, teachers, parents and legal rights and advocacy. SpEdChange.com is one blog.

Homeschooling has many outlets to visit including Homeschoolers Anonymous and Real Life At Home.

oebd.org – features over 100 education blogs

askrandiwhy.com – questions randi weingarten's work as union leader

classsizematter.com

MOVIES RELATED TO EDUCATION

Up the Down Staircase

Won't Back Down

The Breakfast Club

Dangerous Minds

To Sir WIth Love

Little House On The Prairie

Waiting for "Superman"

Freedom Writers

Bad Teacher

Blackboard Jungle

Goodbye, Mr. Chips

BOOKS RELATED TO EDUCATION AND OTHER BOOKS THAT INCLUDE EDUCATION – CONNECTED TOPICS

There are to date over 14,000 books printed on every type of education topic – in every area, including a few – and far too few with fictional settings.

My suggestion is to select a subtopic within education and start reading books about that subject. Do you want to be a teacher? Classroom management and behaviors? Children in charter schools? Or pick an area like American History, Immigration, Trade Jobs to name a few – and seek out chapters of books that relate to education.

Look into education book publishers and review their catalogs. Even if a book is geared to an educator, many are available to parents and the public. Look into books that education courses include as part of required reading.

There are so many ways to read books about education that it is simply impossible to give a fair list here.

IMMIGRATION AND EDUCATION

Should we compare the immigration of the early 1900s to today as a comparison to the involvement of new students into the system?

Should illegal immigrants be included in our system today and in the future?

Should illegal immigrants have jobs in our education system in any arena they wish to work in?

Does our system help or hurt immigrants today by not emphasizing learning English as a primary language?

Should all immigrants be "grouped" together?

Should immigrants take tests on their skills after living here a certain amount of time in regards to reading, writing, math and American history?

Do we really listen to our recent immigrant's needs in education or do we give them what we think they need?

How much of an immigrant's background should we include in a formal education system?

Examples of Legal Cases and Issues Connected with Education and Educators

There are thousands of federal, state and local legal cases tied directly to and with subjects overlapping with the education system. Here is just a brief listing of a few. This area could read like a history book with subtitles including education. Cases involving any type of discrimination like racism, civil rights, anti – semitism, feminism and women's rights, right to choose, learning needs, the rights of Native Americans, Chinese – Americans, Hispanic Americans – all fit here. Many cases deal with funding and put you – a taxpayer – right in the middle – even if you didn't realize it.

This is a small sampling:

Brown vs the Board of Education is probably the most famous education legal case and I think you should learn about it yourself, if you have not already.

Everson vs Board of Education established the limits of the federal government and its connection to religion in regards to education. This Supreme Court case is the basis for many other cases involving policies in the matter of religion – including transportation to private religious schools, curriculum, and funding.

There are multiple cases that involve school districts and higher education institutions that state that in the United States all people shall not be discriminated against or denied the benefits of and education or participation in activities that receive federal funding. They include Grove City College vs. Bell, and Jackson vs Birmingham Board of Education.

Federal and state courts have been deciding the issues of abstinence – only vs comprehensive sex ed for several decades, although it seems as if more are being addressed currently.

There are many court cases involving sex education in various school systems. One of the most recent and followed in the media and by lawmakers nationally took place in California.

In August 2012, parents and physicians sued the Clovis Unified School District in Fresno, California claiming that the district is putting the health of its students at risk by teaching students misinformation and denying them critical instruction by appropriate educators in the field of health, contraception, and condom use.

In May, 2015, Fresno County Superior Court Judge Donald Black decided that California's sex – education law prohibits school districts from indoctrinating students on the need to remain celibate before marriage or educating them that the only safe way to prevent getting pregnant or contracting a sexual disease is to remain abstinent.

Testing makes headlines nationally regarding education. New York Congressman Lee Zeldin introduced in March 2015 an amendment that would allow states to withdraw from the Common Core standards without jeopardizing federal funding.

In May 2015, discrimination took center stage as Asian American Student Groups sued Harvard for Discrimination. A complaint filed by 64 groups against Harvard University alleges that Harvard discriminates against Asian American applicants in admissions. The suit accuses that the University has set quotas to keep the numbers of Asian – American students significantly lower than the quality of their applications merits. It cites SAT exam grades showing that Asian – Americans have to score on average about 140 points higher than white students, 270 points higher than Hispanic students and 450 points higher than other minority students to equal their chances of gaining admission to Harvard.

The complaint was filed with the U.S. Education Department's Office for Civil Rights.

In 2015, there were lawsuits involving physical education, state gun laws that make schools liable in connection to violence and other court cases involving student loans. There are many lawsuits by parents, advocacy groups and individuals ongoing as we go to print.

WWW.SHOWANDTELLFORPARENTS.COM has a list of over 30 cases and is continually updated with legal actions including students and parents versus the education system

If someone has alternative motives for filing complaints that seem to accuse a teacher or administrator of wrongdoings, should they be brought up on charges if their motive is questionable and the accusation proven to be false?

What are Chancellor's Regulations? You can read the many, many pages online and decide if they apply to your needs? The needs of others?

What is mandated reporting? Who are mandated reporters? How does it relate to federal and state social services acts in regard to physical, sexual and emotional abuse and/or neglect?

LESSON PLANS/ACTIVITIES/SCHOOL CALENDAR

What are lesson plans?

Who should decide a lesson plan?

Should lesson plans be universal or personalized?

Who should have input on lesson plans?

Can anyone write a lesson plan? Implement it?

How much of a lesson plan should be planned? Improvised? Totally changed if not working as it is being shared with a class?

Should supervisors have control over lesson plans?

Should lesson plans include input from parents and/or students?

Should schools provide lessons in arts/sports/music and other cultural areas of interest?

How should sports play in the decision making of "higher education?"

Should school provide more assemblies?

Should the school calendar extend into nights? Weekends? All seasons?

Should schools teach sex education? HIV education? Who should be informing students about these subjects? Should teachers be handing out contraception?

Should schools teach about same – sex marriages? Single parent households?

Should schools adapt to custody situations where children are dividing weeks in different households? Which school should be accountable to testing and record keeping?

What are differentiated instructions? Pair and Group Learning?

How do technology skills/equipment/training fit into an education system?

Current Events

The following information regards a principal and a teacher, both working within the New York City Department of Education. Both have been the subjects of a lot of media coverage. I am summarizing details from what has been printed in the New York Post, New York Daily News, the Gothamist, nyrubberroomreporter.blogspot.com, Inside Schools, Daily Mail (UK), Huffington Post, to name a few places where these educators have been reported about. All the information listed below has be printed in more than one area and can be easily found if researched.

Most schools have wonderful staffs, from school nurses, volunteers, suppliers and of course, our teachers and administration. But as in a bunch of grapes, one or two are sour. Here are two examples.

GRETA HAWKINS
Principal
P.S. 90, EDNA COHEN SCHOOL, BROOKLYN

P.S. 90 part of school district 21. Ms. Hawkins has worked as a teacher, then principal for the Department of Education for over 15 years. She has been at P.S. since 2009. During Ms. Hawkins tenure, the following allegations have been made against her and reported publicly:

* threatening to report the parents of misbehaving students to the Administration for Children's Services

*underreporting and filing safety reports

*refusing to account for $3,600 of Title I parent involvement funds

*heard saying remarks like "I'm black. Your previous principal was white and Jewish. More of us are coming."

*harassing staff members so the turnovers in staff are catastrophic and hinder learning

*committing fraud on parent surveys

*buildings understaffed on all levels

The UFT has an unfair labor practice charge against Hawkins regarding a matter pending at the state Public Employment Relations Board and won a grievance against Hawkins in 2013 (uft.org for more information)

Yet, as of May 2015, Hawkins is still receiving a six – figure salary and all benefits awaiting the results of a pending investigation.

SIMON WATTS
TEACHER
P.S. 15, JACKIE ROBINSON SCHOOL, QUEENS

Queens District Attorney Richard Brown's office announced that Simons Watts was a defendant and convicted of second – degree course of sexual conduct against a child, two counts of first – degree sexual abuse, one count of forcible touching, and five counts of endangering the welfare of a child during a two – week trial in Queens Supreme Court in June, 2013. What is concerning is the fact that Watts, according to trial testimony and by all media accounts, had been sexually abusing several children, some multiple times over a three – year period. All were between the ages of eight and 10 – years old. In November, 2013, Queens Supreme Court Justice Michael D. Aloise announced that Watts had been sentenced to 35 yeas in prison.

According to the Canarsie Courier, David Cantor, press secretary at the Department of Education at that time, the DOE had knowledge of three allegations against Watts when he worked for a school in Brooklyn, previous to his tenure in P.S. 15. All but one – for alleged corporal punishment in 2005 – were substantiated. Watts got a letter of reprimand in his file and was twice placed in the old "rubber rooms" while investigations were ongoing.

The following information relates to the riots in Maryland.

BALTIMORE
APRIL 1015
THE DEATH OF FREDDIE GRAY, JR.

I am not here to exonerate or convict any police officer in the death of 25 – year – old Freddie Gray, Jr. while in police custody. I want you to think about how education became an issue during the weeks between the initial incident, the funeral, riots and burning of Baltimore and the ongoing investigations. Television and print media spent hours investigating and interviewing all "informed" sources regarding how an education system failed Freddie Gray and his peers. Yet, we found out that Baltimore spends roughly $15,000 a student in the system, one of the highest amounts per student in this country. Baltimore schools have been the recipient of significant levels of federal and state funding. Students performed on average or slightly worse on standardized state tests. Graduation rates at city schools are below average.

Unfortunately, these results seem common among city schools.

It raises the questions ... Why does a death of a man on the streets of a city, not a school building and not by students or faculty fall into the category of the failure of a school system when "investigated by the media?"

SYRIAN REFUGEES
SUMMER/FALL 2015

During the summer and fall months, many refugees from Syria are immigrating to countries in Europe, particularly Germany. There is a debate ongoing in the United States as to how many, if any refugees we should welcome here. How does it relate to the education system? How much will each refugee cost a taxpayer? Will refugees assimilate into the system easily? Will refugees demand anything from our school administrations?

Bullying/Social Media

There are so many connections of bullying in the system – teacher against student, peers against one another, staff against other staff, parents against staff – the relationships are endless – BUT – the common thread is that usually someone gets hurt and that education gets effected. We, as a society must understand and end bullying of any kind, but we also must stop targeting a school society as if it is the only place where bullying is a constant.

What we can and should think about is how to use our positive tools within a system to help stop bullying of all kinds.

There are many cases of suicides and crimes connected to student and staff bullying. I will share two examples.

According to reports, 12 – year – old Alyssa Morgan of Pleasant Hill, Iowa, committed suicide in April 2015 because she did not feel worthy after being bullied by her peers for being bi – sexual. Her mother, Nicole Morgan reached out to media outlets and shared her daughter's story about how her daughter dreaded going to Southeast Polk High School every day and finding her body. It seems as if this was not the first suicide tied to bullying in the district.

Sometimes bullying leads to inappropriate behaviors and what might seem like innocent fun can turn deadly. Take the case of 17 – year – old Sergi Casper who died in December, 2014 after being bullied. He was wrapped in clear plastic wrap and fell towards a teacher's desk, and as he was sustaining injuries, classmates laughed and ignored his condition. He was later taken to a local hospital where he later passed away.

Social media, including but not limited to Facebook, Twitter and Instagram do not help matters. This is not just about bullying. Are adults not allowed to voice concerns on their private accounts during their own time regarding a frustration connected to a work – related situation? What about the use of photos – should educators, students and parents be judged on what they do, where they go and who they associate with during their free time?

Falsifying Grades on School Reviews/on Tests/Adult Evaluations and Cheating

As we go to press, probably the biggest scandal to date has made front page headlines nationally. In April, 2015, 11 of 12 defendants in an Atlanta public schools cheating scandal were convicted of racketeering and a slew of other charges not limited to making false statements and altering and fabricating scores for at least four years between 2005 and 2009. Later that month, the judge reduced three sentences and the penalties are still pending. Claims of over 200,000 test answers were tampered with on all levels of staff.

Falsifying paperwork is not new and not limited the education system. But are we teaching our minors the right values when we alter accurate details? Who does it benefit? Does this relate to affirmative action? Athletes applying and getting admitted to universities on their physical abilities rather than their academic achievements? Here is a separate, yet connected topic with much debate and research to be looked into.

THE FUTURE OF EDUCATION

How can we improve education?

Should education remain a government responsibility?

Should education be run like a private business? Competitive?

Should we change the school calendar?

Should the school system provide services for students with two parents that work full – time – as a "baby – sitting" service?

What is the future of unions within the education system?

Will evaluations change? Should they?

When should we see positive movement towards success in the system?

Should we develop a new type of schooling?

Do we need to purchase new supplies and equipment – an example – less books and more technological equipment to educate?

What cost – effective measure do we need to utilize as we encounter rising education costs in a debt – based society?

How are we providing in our schools the tools needed for job growth in our country in the future?

Did you know that there are currently over 3,000 national, regional, and state education organizations providing information and assistance and anyone who has concerns and interests related to education – based topics. I suggest you look into them and compare information and memberships. Most provide resources and staff to assist you.

Presidential election of 2016 – How will education issues play into who is elected at all levels of government? Will legislation like NY Education tax credit play a role and set state trends? Politicians are tying education issues to immigration legislation like the Dream Act.

What should the role of religious leaders like Archbishop Timothy Cardinal Dolan. Rev. Al Sharpton, and organizations like NAACP, ACORN, Interfaith Worker Justice, The Expectations Project and their leader Nicole Baker Fulgham try to help develop the connections of religion and the need for improving public schools, the Inner – City Muslim Action Network, led by Rami Nashashibi in Chicago and many other organizations and leaders. There are simply too many to name. Who are the groups and leaders that work for universal solutions or simply personal fame and fortune? Who wants to work as a team and who wants to just place blame?

Check out for yourselves and perhaps inquire about membership, receiving regular newsletters and updated information. Do you see patterns? Are they actually working with school students, parents and teachers in a comfortable environment?

Where should parent accountability fall in the future of education? Do guardians need report cards and evaluations like students, educators, administrators and school building themselves?

Should we create new school calendars?

Should school buildings continue to provide breakfast/lunch/snacks?

Should school building be allowed to be used to political polling centers? Should religious institutions be allowed to rent auditoriums and space – even when school business hours are closed?

Should we look into higher ed/college costs/student loans? Are advanced degrees needed? How about the connection of political activism on campus as it relates directly with education?

Should studies be conducted to relate college acceptance to sports and not grades/affirmative action/ courses and professors?

Does class size matter? What ratio is a successful student to educator in class? Should every class have aides? Paraprofessionals?

Education Resource Organizations Directory

The Education Resource Organizations Directory (EROD) contains information on more than 3,000 national, regional, and state education organizations including many associations that provide information and assistance on a broad range of education – related topics.

As you see, you can review each question and seem more confused, frustrated or uneducated. Digest this section slowly. Read, and reread. Remember, if the answers were so easy to respond to, our education system would be different.

ARE YOU A CRITIC OR TEAM PLAYER?

Many like to talk and complain, few take the steps to work with others and find some solutions

Ending this book on a high note – the following short essays by respected leaders in their fields offer ideas that you might find thought provoking

I am not going to comment whether or not they are might thoughts – i want to work with you, not tell you

Enclosed are two afterwards that each represent the work and views of people who are trying to make a positive impact on education. I may or may not agree with them ... I compliment them on putting words into actions and making people think and want to learn more.

CHANGE THINKING AND ANSWERS WILL FOLLOW

By Wally Hauck, Phd, Certified Speaking Professional and President of Optimum Leadership

If education needs significant (not incremental) improvement how does significant improvement occur? When we truly want to make a difference in something what should we do? Should we put in more effort, more money, more time, or some other resources?

Improvement in anything occurs from a change in the process. Significant improvement occurs when we change our thinking. Our educational system requires such a change in thinking. Significant improvement has not occurred for years because the same level of thinking dominates and that thinking is flawed.

In 1942 the first class of African American flyers graduated from the Tuskegee Army Airfield in Tuskegee Alabama. (Black History Month – The Tuskegee Airmen, 2015) The Tuskegee Airmen (Redtails) changed their thinking and were able to achieve amazing results. The graduates were trained to fly support for long range bombers over Europe during World War II.

When the Tuskegee airmen were assigned to bomber escort duty, the "system" was redefined as a "Bomber/Fighter" system that rewarded everyone for getting the bombers there and back with a minimum of loss. It was Captain Benjamin Davis' idea to change to this strategy. This new thinking changed behavior (the fighters stayed close to the bomber formations) and therefore changed results. Thanks to the interaction of their skills, the leadership of Captain Davis, and a new way of thinking, every bomber made it home safely in over 2,000 missions.

Our Flawed Thinking

Here are a few examples of the flawed thinking that currently dominates our school systems. We focus on teaching students instead enabling them to learn. We steal their freedom of choice. Our country was founded on the concept of freedom and yet we steal it away with our policies and bureaucratic methods. We don't give students the freedom to choose what they want to learn. We don't provide freedom to teachers to optimize their skills. The curriculum is set by others who supposedly know more than all of us about what we need.

This lack of appreciation for freedom in learning results in treating students like empty vessels that need to be filled with certain facts and concepts. These concepts and facts are carefully selected by omniscient teachers and administrators and we use standardized tests to measure the amount of information students have retained in their vessels. What do these tests actually measure? Is it the quality of teaching? Is it the quality of the student's study habits? Is it the quality of the text book? It's assumed these tests measure something important. They do not. Furthermore, the testing results show either a flat line or a slow failure.

Our educational system fails to appreciate the idea that learning occurs at different rates with different students for different reasons. It instead treats all students the same and groups them in the same age groups and often with an irrelevant capability measure such as Intelligent Quotient (IQ). Students end up feeling frustration and boredom and these feelings are barriers to learning.

Our system puts more importance on compliance to these standardized tests and the predetermined curriculum than to what students really need to optimize their own personal learning and become excellent problem solvers and critical thinkers. Our priorities are upside down because our thinking is flawed. We are immersed in the "knowledge age" and have not yet outgrown our "industrial age" thinking.

The "New" Thinking

Our new thinking must recognize that the variation in learning can only be managed by the student themselves (not be a tyrannical bureaucracy). Our new thinking and our new system must, not just allow but encourage, all students to manage their own learning. The new thinking must also acknowledge that learning is an active process which can only be managed by the student. Learning is not memorization. Only then can we hope to build life – long learners.

Just as Captain Davis offered new thinking for the Tuskegee Airmen, there are two geniuses, who never met each other, can begin to give us hope that significant improvement can be achieved in education. Dr. W. Edwards Deming (The Deming Institute Home Page, 2015) and Dr. Reuven Feuerstein (Feuerstein Institute, 2015) each offer us exciting new ways of thinking.

Deming was a management consultant who reinforced the learning model of Plan – Do – Check – Act (PDCA). PDCA enables anyone to improve their processes and its use over time can create significant improvements.

Feuerstein was a psychologist who developed a method to uncover an individual child's unique learning process. He developed this working with children who were psychologically impacted by the World War II Holocaust. Once the learning process was uncovered the child could then manage his/her own learning. The management of this process could be continuously improved using PDCA.

Deming and Feuerstein give us a new model which allows the child to take responsibility for their own learning. The teacher no longer needs to pour information into the "empty vessel." Now the teacher facilitates the continuous improvement of the individual learning process in partnership with the student who becomes an active leader of his/her own learning. He/she can then apply this skill to create a productive life. Testing can be used but not for compliance. Instead the student can choose their own testing to measure how well he/she is learning what they want to learn. Testing becomes a tool for the student to apply PDCA to their learning process. Our current thinking is blocking these new ideas.

Captain Davis helped the Tuskegee Airmen achieve significant improvement and it helped change the world for the better. Deming and Feuerstein can help us do the same for education. We can each challenge the current thinking model which dominates our education system by being open to a new way of thinking and it will lead to a new way of behaving which will lead to the significant results we all desire.

Wally Hauck, PhD, CSP is a student of Dr. W. Edwards Deming's System of Profound Knowledge and firmly believes Deming's work will reinvigorate organizations that suffer from lackluster performance. Wally holds a doctorate in organizational leadership from Warren National University, a Master of Business Administration in finance from Iona College, and a bachelor's degree in philosophy from the University of Pennsylvania. Wally is a Certified Speaking Professional or CSP. For 19 years his consulting firm, Optimum Leadership, has consulted with dozens of organizations and coached hundreds of individuals in improving leadership skills, employee engagement, and performance. Wally has taught Organizational Change and Development at the University of New Haven in Connecticut. Wally lives in Connecticut with his wife Lorraine.

TEACH YOUR CHILDREN WELL

by Laurie Cardoza – Moore – Th.D, President of Proclaiming Justice to the Nations

Following the horrific attacks on 9/11, I began to ask, like most Americans, what happened to our country. As I researched and talked to experts, the issues of radical Islam and the attacks on America and Israel became extremely personal to me. In response, I founded Proclaiming Justice to the Nations, a non – profit organization dedicated to educating Christians about their biblical responsibility to stand with and for the people and land of Israel. I established PJTN as a powerful Christian voice for Israel in the media using my years of experience in broadcasting and film. Christians were for the most part silent during the first Holocaust, I believe we cannot be silent again.

Little did I realize I would be fighting anti – Semitism in my very own backyard. For the last twenty – five years, we have resided in Williamson County, a county with a long tradition of being one of the top ten most conservative counties in the U.S, a county in the very center of the Bible belt, a county where Christians should not stand by in silence. I discovered that behind our backs, a liberal school board agenda had taken hold and was indoctrinating our children. Several controversial incidents and troubling educational materials have been cause for great alarm.

Anti – Semitism in a Pearson published textbook

In November of 2012, a concerned Williamson County parent contacted PJTN about a controversial human geography textbook (The Cultural Landscape) being used in her son's high school. The immediate problem involved a section under the title, "Terrorism by Individuals and Organizations," that asks students to consider the following question on why terrorism has increased:

"If a Palestinian suicide bomber kills several dozen Israeli teenagers in a Jerusalem restaurant, is that an act of terrorism or wartime retaliation against Israeli government policies and army actions?"

During the same class, an anti – Israel handout and a guest speaker influenced her son to question his faith and the accuracy of the Bible concerning Israel and her rights to her ancient homeland. This led to the concerned parent contacting me. It was also discovered that another student had remarked, that "had he not taken the class, he wouldn't have known about the dangerous Zionist agenda."

Meetings with the school's faculty led nowhere, so I filed an official complaint with the school district requesting the textbook's removal due to the highly objectionable statement. With the help of several parents, nearly a dozen other objectionable passages, descriptions and word choices were also found in the book. Not only was the textbook anti – Semitic and anti – Israel, but it was replete with anti – Christian, anti – Western and pro – Marxist propaganda as well.

Despite gathering over 1300 signatures protesting the book, other parents' outcries, and repeated school board meetings, Williamson County Schools Director, Mike Looney, encouraged the board to vote to continue using the book. Looney defended the use of this textbook because it had been used for several years with no one ever filing a formal complaint. He further stated, "I personally don't get that anti – Semitic perspective from reading the question in context. I respect other people's viewpoints and understand they might read it differently." He also felt that one passage in a 500 – page book could not justify discontinuing its use.

The Nashville Jewish Federation supported PJTN's leadership on this matter and agreed that the textbook needed to be removed and issued this statement:

"To create moral equivalency between specific acts of terror and legitimate territorial disputes that are political in nature serves to legitimize wanton and premeditated violence against innocent civilian victims. To further allow distorted, unbalanced and prejudicial content to stand as a form of academic inquiry is a perversion of our educational system and a disservice to all the children who learn in that system."

– Mark Freedman, Jewish Federation Executive Director

In October 2013, I took the issue to the Tennessee State Legislature where my advocacy against anti – Semitism is well recognized among the state's legislators. In a state that has passed several strong pro – Israel resolutions, legislators shared my concern about the material being presented to students. I testified before The Tennessee Senate Education Committee to address their concerns about this textbook material. This testimony was instrumental in the Tennessee legislature introducing bills this year related to textbook issues.

The Double Standard in the Williamson County School District

Mr. Looney and other county officials refuse to acknowledge the detrimental effect of textbook and curriculum materials containing subtle and not so subtle expressions of anti – Semitism and Jew hatred. Under his leadership, the doctrine of anti – Semitism has permeated into the students and faculty of the school district.

For example, in September 2013, two male students at a Williamson County Middle School stood at the front of my car giving me a "Heil Hitler" salute in response to a "Defend and Protect America and Israel" bumper sticker on my vehicle. After contacting the school's principal to make her aware of the incident, it was discovered that the students were from nearby Ravenwood High School. Despite identification of the students from viewing the school's security camera tape, no action has been taken to address this incident. To date, my request regarding disciplinary action continues to go unanswered by Ravenwood's principal.

This is the same high school that in 2009 permitted a Palestinian Arab booth at the school's Cultural Heritage Fair to distribute venomous anti – Semitic propaganda. The "Arab – Palestinian" booth was displaying anti – Israel hate propaganda that included "doctored" pictures of Israeli soldiers shooting babies and the security fence labeled as an "apartheid wall."

This year, during the school's Cultural Heritage Week, Muslim students claimed offense because of a pamphlet that was being distributed by a local Jewish organization at the event. The pamphlet contained accurate information about the anti – Semitic hatred that is taught to children in U.S. funded Palestinian schools. The double standard and hypocrisy at Ravenwood High School and the school district at – large should outrage students and parents.

The pamphlet in question was published by "StandWithUs (SWU), an organization that is dedicated to publishing accurate educational information about the Arab – Israeli conflict for use in a high school/university environment. On a page that describes the problem in the Arab culture under, "Teaching Peace", it describes the incitement to hatred and violence against Israel and Jews that is pervasive in Arab/Palestinian media, schools, and mosques. "In fact, it is this incitement that disturbed then Senator Hillary Clinton in 2007, and that continues to disturb peace makers because the incitement leads to violence and has always been an obstacle to peace," stated Roz Rothstein, President of SWU.

The truth...this particular pamphlet is entirely educational and appropriate for this event. It is PJTN's opinion that in Williamson County and at a school like Ravenwood, where anti – Semitic incidents have occurred and anti – Semitic textbook materials have been found, this educational pamphlet, should be required reading. To provide accurate information about the conflict in the Middle East should be welcomed in the "educational" environment of a high school. Accurate and unbiased resources about the Middle East allow our children to use their critical thinking skills concerning this ongoing conflict.

Double Standards and Double – Speech

This situation leads me to ask the question, what are we teaching the immigrants that come to Tennessee, especially from the Middle East? Israel is our only true friend and ally in the Middle East. We, as a Judeo/Christian nation, share the same values of freedom and faith as our Jewish brethren in Israel. It is that freedom that allows people of all faiths and nationalities to live without fear of persecution not only in our country, but in our county as well. It is critical that we provide accurate and unbiased textbooks to the immigrants that make Williamson County their home. I fear if we do not, we may find similar horrific justification for terrorist attacks here.

Finally, as a result of this whole issue, a deeper – rooted problem has surfaced. What does it say about our local leaders when school officials will censor pamphlets with accurate information that Muslims find offensive but refuse to remove inaccurate anti – Semitic/anti – Israel and anti – Western textbooks at the request of Christian and Jewish parents?

This obvious double standard must not stand unchallenged and must be dealt with at the voting booth. This growing threat further illustrates how critically important local elections are, especially when those elected leaders will be influencing the future direction of our nation. With elections quickly approaching, I hope more Williamson County citizens will join me in some crucially needed "spring cleaning" on this school board, that refuses to uphold the values of the citizens of this great county.

Ironically, as a result of the national and international media attention generated by PJTN, Pearson Publishers agreed with the parents and removed the anti – Semitic quote from future editions of the Human Geography textbook. This is certainly a small and important victory, but the battle continues.

To save our country, we must retake it one small county, one small election at a time. As we have slept, the progressive agenda has penetrated every strata of our government and our educational system. It is a long road ahead but we can no longer afford not to walk it.

Laurie Cardoza – Moore is founder and President of Proclaiming Justice To The Nations (PJTN) and Special Envoy to the UN for the World Council of Independent Christian Churches (WCICC). An accomplished veteran of the many facets of 'media' Laurie has been part of over 500 film and video productions as on – screen talent and producer.

With over twenty – five years experience in private enterprise, grassroots mobilization and community leadership, Laurie's mission through PJTN and WCICC is to educate Christians around the globe to stand with Israel and our Jewish brethren against the rise of the "new" anti – Semitism.

ACKNOWLEDGMENTS

There are many to thank when a published piece of work is complete. This book took many years to finish.

First of all, this book could not have been the success it is today without the dedication of many, many teachers, administrators, students and their families. Those in particular who helped me personally during my days in the classroom and since have been the source of encouragement to continue my quest for change to achieve success in our education system. Many asked me not to mention them by name. It is a shame that they fear any repercussions from assisting in telling the truths and trying to improve what seems to be a failing system. What a shame, as they pay taxes, dues and have such an important role in shaping our country's future.

I also need to thank those in the legal system who have worked with me for many years, realizing that I had known my facts, had the strength and when I felt down, encouraged me to continue.

I wish to thank Ann Schockett, President of the NYS Federation of Republican Women, Elizabeth L. Faenza, best – selling author, Wally Hauck, President of Optimum Leadership and Laurie Cardoza – Moore and everyone on staff at Proclaiming Justice to the Nations for their input and ability to use their expertise to help tell the facts and try to make change as well.

Acquaintances are many – friends are few. For the few who knew some of what has happened over the past few years and helped me with my desire to make positive change and educate the public – thank you. They include Dan, Susie and Eli, Stacey and Howie, Shely and Jack, Vivien and Alan and of course, Ellen and Jeff. This book could not have been completed at any level without the constant support of Phil and Louise.

Finally to my family, Muriel and Leonard, Peter, Vita and Steve, Rebekah and to the only person all this is for ... Michael.

Cindy